Meet the United Pentecostal Church International

Written by

David Bernard

C. A. Brewer

P. D. Buford

Dan Butler

Gary Erickson

J. L. Hall

T. M. Jackson

Edwin Judd

Ralph Reynolds

Dan Segraves

This book was designed for personal or group study.

WORD AFLAME® PUBLICATIONS

PENTECOSTAL PUBL
8855 DUNN ROAD
HAZELWOOD, MO 63042-
www.upci.org/wap
www.pentecostalpublishing.com

Word Aflame Elective Series

Alive in the Spirit
Bible Doctrines—Foundation of the Church
The Bible—Its Origin and Use
Building Family Relationships
The Christian Man
The Christian Parent
The Christian Woman
The Christian Youth
Facing the Issues
Financial Planning for Successful Living
Friendship, Courtship, and Marriage
The Holy Spirit
Life's Choices
A Look at Pentecostal Worship
A Look at Stewardship
Meet the United Pentecostal Church International
Purpose at Sunset
Salvation—Key to Eternal Life
Spiritual Growth and Maturity
Spiritual Leadership and Successful Soulwinning
Strategy for Life for Singles and Young Adults
Values That Last
WHY? A Study of Christian Standards
Your New Life

Pentecostal Digital Reference Library

Volume 4—Word Aflame Elective Series

Editorial Staff

R. M. Davis . . . . Editor
P. D. Buford . . . . Associate Editor

Reprint History: 1989, 1992, 1995, 1997, 2000, 2004,
(revised) 2008, 2009, 2010
ISBN 1-56722-056-8

CURRICULUM COMMITTEE: James E. Boatman, Donald Bryan, P. D. Buford, Daniel L. Butler, Richard M. Davis, Gary D. Erickson, Jack C. Garrison, G. W. Hassebrock, Vernon D. McGarvey, David S. Norris, David L. Reynolds, Charles A. Rutter, R. L. Wyser.

Foreword

David K. Bernard
General Superintendent
United Pentecostal Church International

The United Pentecostal Church International (UPCI) is the largest Oneness Pentecostal organization in the world. It was formed in 1945 by a merger of the Pentecostal Assemblies of Jesus Christ, which had 346 churches, and the Pentecostal Church Incorporated, which had 175 churches. From this beginning of 521 churches, by 2009 the UPCI had grown to 4,330 churches in the United States and Canada and 30,000 churches worldwide (including daughter works and preaching points). It is now represented in 190 nations, with a worldwide constituency of three million. Internationally, the UPCI is on a trajectory to double in ten years.

The headquarters of the UPCI is World Evangelism Center in Hazelwood, Missouri, a suburb of St. Louis. It houses the offices of Church Administration, the Pentecostal Publishing House, and eight divisions— Apostolic Man, Education, Foreign Missions, Home Missions, Ladies Ministries, Publications, Sunday School, and Youth. Publications of the UPCI include the *Pentecostal Herald* (official periodical), the *Forward* (periodical for ministers), Word Aflame Press books, and Word Aflame Publications curriculum. The UPCI operates Urshan Graduate School of Theology and has endorsed seven Bible colleges in the U.S. and Canada including one for Spanish speakers. In addition, the UPCI has endorsed six ministry projects—a liberal arts college, an online ministerial training network, an adoption agency, a children's home, a residency for troubled young men, and a ministry to alcohol and drug abusers.

As stated in Article I of its General Constitution, the mission of the UPCI is "to carry the whole gospel to the whole world by the whole church." The whole gospel is the good news of salvation by grace through faith based on the atoning death, burial, and resurrection of Jesus Christ, which is applied by repentance from sin, water baptism by immersion in the name of Lord Jesus Christ for the remission of sins, and the baptism of the Holy Ghost with the initial sign of speaking in tongues as the Spirit gives utterance. After receiving this wonderful experience of salvation, Christians are to grow in grace and knowledge and to pursue holiness both inwardly and outwardly.

As Oneness Pentecostals, the key to our identity is the message, experience, and life of the apostles and the New Testament church. By maintaining and proclaiming our apostolic identity, we will enjoy unity while embracing diversity, continue on a trajectory of growth, and minister effectively in the twenty-first century.

I would like to thank the editor of Word Aflame Publications, Richard M. Davis, and the associate editor, P. D. Buford, for developing this book. It is a valuable resource both for members of the UPCI and for those outside the movement. Through this study, we can gain a better understanding of the uniqueness, significance, and operations of the United Pentecostal Church International and the worldwide Apostolic Pentecostal movement.

Contents

The First-Century Church

1

*Beloved, when I gave all diligence to write
unto you of the common salvation, it was needful
for me to write unto you, and exhort you that ye
should earnestly contend for the faith which was
once delivered unto the saints.*

Jude 3

Start with the Scriptures

Matthew 7:24-27   I Corinthians 3:11
Acts 1-28   Ephesians 2:20-22

The first-century church was magnificent at its birth and mighty in its early existence. From about 120 persons in the upper room it grew to over 3,000 in one day, but its strength lay neither in numbers nor in material possessions. The early church knew nothing of hymnals or stained glass windows. There were no carpeted floors or padded pews where the early Christians gathered to pray. The church of that day was more than a vibrant force; it was a tidal wave of power that swept all before it.

If we would know what the church is meant to be today, then we must examine the church as described by God's Word, the Bible. The divine pattern for the church remains the same today as it was in those first years after Christ's ascension into heaven. People's ideas of Christianity have certainly changed, but God's purposes can never be altered.

Religious movements have come and gone. Many movements have flourished for a time, reached a certain maturity, begun to wither, languished, and finally they died. The pattern has often been repeated. If such a movement should survive, it is often just an empty shell of the original.

There is one notable exception to the common trend. Jesus Christ told the apostle Peter, "Upon this rock I will build my church; and the gates of hell shall not prevail against it" (Matthew 16:18). Christ came to establish a church with a supernatural origin and a mandate to serve all mankind. Neither time nor circumstances could alter the divine blueprint. The church would be built by the great Architect Himself. It could not fail, for He could not fail. The resurrected Christ encouraged His disciples: "All power is given unto me in heaven and in earth" (Matthew 28:18).

The Foundation of the Church

Supporting the entire building above it, a foundation provides the necessary stability. No structure can be any stronger than its foundation. As Jesus explained in the Sermon on the Mount, a house needs to be built upon something solid enough to bear every adverse circumstance. (See Matthew 7:24-27.)

Destined to be battered by the world, accused by the devil, and tempted by the flesh, the church of the first century did stand the test. Almost from its inception the church suffered persecution from religious authorities. At Jerusalem there were three attempts to snuff out the light of the gospel by fierce opposition. "The first is described in Acts, Chapter 4; the second in Acts 5:17-42; the third in Acts 7:38-8:3. But none of these persecutions could stop the victorious progress of the Christian Church" (Lars P. Qualben, *A History of the Christian Church*, Thomas Judson and Sons, New York, 1960, page 41).

The foundation was all important. No organization could have withstood such pressures and still have grown stronger without God's direct involvement. No human institution, however gifted, could have so transformed the pagan world of that day.

"For other foundation can no man lay than that is laid, which is Jesus Christ" (I Corinthians 3:11).

The church was reared on Christ, the one and only foundation. All else is sinking sand. The Almighty Himself is the strength of the whole superstructure. God's Spirit (the same Spirit that dwelt in Christ) permeates each and every believer. The church, an edifice constructed at great sacrifice, has risen to astound the world. Believers "are built upon the foundation of the apostles and prophets, Jesus Christ himself being the chief corner stone; in whom all the building fitly framed together groweth unto an holy temple in the Lord: in whom ye also are builded together for an habitation of God through the Spirit" (Ephesians 2:20-22).

It is the indwelling Spirit within the church which unifies and strengthens the whole. (See Ephesians 4:3-6.) Wherever believers are founded firmly on the Lord, the Rock of Ages, there is a love for truth and a love for one another. All races and nationalities blend perfectly together in Christ. Indeed, "the love of God is shed abroad in our hearts by the Holy Ghost which is given unto us" (Romans 5:5).

The early church was alive and well. Its members had implicit faith in God, and they prayed fervently with times of fasting. They preached of a resurrected Christ who performed miracles in their midst. Even their enemies witnessed to the power of God in their ministry, stating, "These that have turned the world upside down are come hither also" (Acts 17:6).

The Founding of the Church

Everything about the first century church speaks of the supernatural. God had the church in mind before the foundation of the world. (See Ephesians 1:4.) Christians are a chosen race and a royal priesthood. They are a "peculiar people" intended to proclaim God's wonderful power and goodness to men (I Peter 2:9-10).

As Jesus prophesied to His disciples, the witness of the church was to begin at Jerusalem. That city, so privileged and yet so guilty before God, was the first to receive the gospel. Repentance and remission of sins would eventually be preached in the name of Jesus among all nations (Luke 24:47), but the message of salvation began at the very site that God had chosen.

The exact time for the founding of the church was also chosen. Jesus said, "Tarry ye in the city of Jerusalem, until ye be endued with power from on high" (Luke 24:49). The disciples probably wondered when this outpouring would take place. How long must they wait? Would the promised Holy Ghost be long in coming? Would God answer prayer in the evening as He had for Elijah on Mount Carmel?

When God chose to send the Holy Spirit, He deliberately determined to make the event widely known. As in the case of the apostle Paul's conversion, "This thing was not done in a corner" (Acts

26:26). God chose a busy time, a festive time. The city of Jerusalem was crowded with Jews and proselytes from many nations. They had gathered to celebrate Pentecost, one of the three religious celebrations that Jews were expected to attend in Jerusalem.

If the fire of the Holy Ghost was to fall on the Jewish community, then certainly this was an appropriate time. The heat of that flame would easily take the gospel into Asia. Africa and Europe would also be touched by that mighty gospel blaze.

"And when the day of Pentecost was fully come . . ." (Acts 2:1). The special day arrived of which the prophet Joel had spoken (Joel 2:28-31). The outpouring of the Holy Ghost on the waiting disciples as recorded in Acts 2 marked the beginning of the church age. If ever God marked off an event as momentous, then this was one of those events. The first supernatural sign was a sound of a mighty wind (Moffatt in his translation called it "a mighty blast"). The second sign was cloven tongues: "And there appeared unto them cloven tongues like as of fire, and it sat upon each of them" (Acts 2:3). The third powerful sign was that of speaking in tongues. Each and every disciple spoke in different languages "as the Spirit gave them utterance" (Acts 2:4).

The one sign that consistently appears throughout the Book of Acts when people received the Holy Spirit is speaking in tongues. (See Acts 10:46; 19:6.) On the Day of Pentecost, speaking in tongues amazed the multitude that had gathered (Acts 2:6-8). And it is still the sign that confounds many scoffers and the skeptics.

If Satan had been perplexed by Calvary, he must have been thoroughly confounded by Pentecost. Here were about one hundred twenty Galileans all speaking in various languages about "the wonderful works of God" (Acts 2:11). A large crowd gathered to see and to hear the disciples. It must have been one of the worst of times for Satan. Peter, whom he had tried to sift as wheat, actually stood and preached with a powerful anointing. The multitude was moved by conviction. Large numbers began to respond. Before the day was over, about three thousand people had been baptized and added to the church.

The Fervency of the Church

Like a blazing torch, the church of the first century lit up the dark recesses and shadowed corners of men's souls. The apostle Peter declared that the Lord had called His people "out of darkness into his marvellous light" (I Peter 2:9). Defending himself to the Jews at Antioch, the apostle Paul stated, "For so hath the Lord commanded us, saying, I have set thee to be a light of the Gentiles, that thou shouldest be for salvation unto the ends of the earth" (Acts 13:47).

The church saw its mission as reaching every individual with the gospel. Paul, the great missionary spokesman, wrote, "I am debtor both to the Greeks, and to the Barbarians; both to the wise, and to the unwise" (Romans 1:14). Without missions boards, Bible schools, or modern methods of communication, the early Christians took the gospel message wherever they went.

Perhaps it was the very simplicity of the lifestyle of each Christian that made the task easier. Unencumbered by what we consider conveniences, the disciples spread the gospel by means of their personal testimonies. "And they, continuing daily with one accord in the temple, and breaking bread from house to house, did eat their meat with gladness and singleness of heart, praising God, and having favour with all the people. And the Lord added to the church daily such as should be saved" (Acts 2:46-47).

Somehow those first-century Christians grasped the true significance of their salvation experience. They were enthralled with the gospel and described their spiritual conversion as being "born again," "transformed," "regenerated" or "born from above." Christ was their first love, their everlasting king. Many of them may have been stricken by poverty or even shackled by slavery, but their enthusiasm seemed unbounded.

The word *gospel* stands for "good news" or "glad tidings." In a world enslaved by sin, the gospel (from the Anglo-Saxon *god-spell*, meaning "God-story") was truly a marvelous proclamation, telling of the divine plan to redeem mankind through Jesus Christ. The earth needed such a message from heaven. Sinners needed to hear the glad news, the glorious revelation "that God was in Christ, reconciling the world unto himself, not imputing their trespasses unto them" (II Corinthians 5:19).

Oh, how those early Christians responded to the preaching of the gospel! Not only did they obey the apostolic message by repenting and being baptized in the name of Jesus Christ (Acts 2:38, 41; 8:12, 38; 16:15, 33; 18:8; 19:5), they also shared the truth wherever they went. They became flaming evangels. Someone has said, "As Satan tried to stamp out the fire, he simply scattered sparks and spread the flames." Energized by the Holy Ghost, an inexhaustible source of power, believers were white hot in their fervency and in their faith.

The Faith of the Church

In many different respects the first-century church was remarkable. The believers of that day were unshakeable in their faith towards God, and their view of the divine purpose was singularly unclouded. They rejoiced when they were persecuted; they sang songs when they were imprisoned. The early Christians had almost a reckless disregard for possessions. In Jerusalem, for instance, they sold their lands and houses, laying the money at the apostles' feet.

Almost everywhere the Christian missionaries went there seemed to be a riot or a revival (and sometimes both). In Samaria under Philip's ministry, unclean spirits, screaming and shouting, were cast out, while those people who were palsied or crippled were healed. (See Acts 8:6-7.) After nearly the whole city of Antioch in Pisidia turned out to hear Paul and Barnabas, and many Gentiles received the gospel, persecution forced them out of that area. (See Acts 13:44-50.) These same two missionaries barely escaped stoning at Iconium, and at Lystra Paul was, in fact, stoned and left for dead. The very next day Paul and Barnabas were on their way to preach at Derbe. And, not much later on, with astounding courage, "They returned again to Lystra, and to Iconium, and Antioch" (Acts 14:21).

Although the first-century church was not without problems (such as the contentions that arose over circumcision of the Gentiles and the eating of meats offered to idols), the missionary effort flourished. In the second and the third of these great undertakings of Paul and his helpers, the work of God was advanced in Europe. The door of faith opened churches in such key cities as Philippi, Thessalonica, Corinth, and Ephesus. Luke, summarizing the powerful impact of the gospel on these population centers, made such statements as, "So mightily grew the word of God and prevailed" (Acts 19:20).

It was not only Paul and his fellow missionaries who took a courageous stand for Christ. A wonderful transformation had taken place in the lives of all those who had been filled with the Spirit. That

14

experience had changed the followers of Christ. From being sometimes dispirited and too often fearful, they became daring in their proclamation of truth.

"Now when they saw the boldness of Peter and John, and perceived that they were unlearned and ignorant men, they marvelled; and they took knowledge of them, that they had been with Jesus" (Acts 4:13).

"And when they had prayed, the place was shaken where they were assembled together; and they were all filled with the Holy Ghost, and they spake the word of God with boldness" (Acts 4:31).

From being people who had hidden in fear behind closed doors, the disciples changed and went everywhere preaching Jesus. Christ was the theme of their thinking and the anthem of their souls. Little else mattered. "For I determined," Paul wrote, "not to know any thing among you, save Jesus Christ, and him crucified" (I Corinthians 2:2).

All of the twelve apostles were practical men. At least four of them had been fishermen and one a publican. Certainly, when they spoke, their words were factual and authoritative, for all of them had been companions of Christ and had witnessed His resurrection. (See Acts 1:21-22.)

Who can question the sincerity of these men who had left all to follow Jesus and who had risked their lives to preach the gospel? The traditional view is that John was the only apostle to die naturally, after being banished to the Isle of Patmos. All the others suffered martyrdom.

There is no need to doubt as to what the apostles taught. Their testimonies are plainly recorded in the Gospels, in the Book of Acts, in the Epistles, and in the Book of Revelation. If there is confusion regarding the apostles' teaching, it arises from those who fail to take their words at face value.

During His earthly ministry Jesus gave His disciples power to heal the sick and cast out demons, but the full truth of His nature had been beyond their comprehension. It all seemed a bit mysterious to them until after the resurrection. (See John 14:5-9.) Then He opened their understanding (Luke 24:45).

After the resurrection the apostles never questioned the authority of Christ. With absolute confidence they called Him "Lord and God." (See John 20:28; Acts 10:36.) They worshiped Him as their sovereign King.

Writing his Gospel in the last quarter of the first century, John focused his attention on Christ's heavenly origin rather than His earthly origin. "All things were made by him," John reported, "and without him was not any thing made that was made" (John 1:3).

Affirmations of Christ's grandeur and His excellent character are stated throughout the New Testament. One after another of the apostles testified to His redeeming love. His spotless life was an inspiration to every convert to live apart from the pollutions of this world.

Certainly the apostles were correct in baptizing all their converts in the name of Jesus. As Paul explained, there is no other name which could suffice, for none other than Jesus was crucified for the sins of mankind. (See I Corinthians 1:13; Romans 6:3-4.) Lest there be any doubt, Paul stated, "And whatsoever ye do in word or deed, do all in the name of the Lord Jesus, giving thanks to God and the Father by him" (Colossians 3:17).

Baptism for the first-century Christian was far more than a ritual or ordinance of the church. When baptism was administered in the name of Jesus Christ, the convert understood that his sins were actually being remitted. (See Acts 2:38; Luke 24:47; Acts 22:16.) Of course, faith in Christ's sacrificial death was essential, as was repentance, but the early church knew well what Christ had stated in His commission. (See Mark 16:15-16.) At Jerusalem (Acts 2:38, 41), Samaria (Acts 8:12, 15), Caesarea (Acts 10:48), Ephesus (Acts 19:1-5), and Damascus (Acts 22:16), the apostles emphatically taught and commanded their converts to be baptized in the name of Jesus Christ.

The Bible teaches explicitly that the early Christians did repent, they were baptized in the name of Jesus, and they did receive the Holy Ghost with the evidence of speaking in other tongues. Acts 2:47 says that "the Lord added to the church daily such as should be saved." This plan was effective, for it was designed by God Himself. Nothing else has ever approached it or will ever replace it. At Pentecost, the first great spiritual outpouring for the church, Peter declared, "For the promise is unto you, and to your children, and to all that are afar off, even as many as the Lord our God shall call" (Acts 2:39).

Test Your Knowledge

1. _____ _____ is the true foundation of the church.

2. The witness of the church was to begin at _____.

3. Pentecost was one of the religious celebrations that _____ were expected to attend in Jerusalem.

4. The prophet _____ had spoken of the outpouring of the Holy Ghost.

5. The first supernatural sign in the upper room was a mighty _____.

6. The word _____ stands for "good news" or "glad tidings."

7. In _____, under Philip's ministry, unclean spirits were cast out.

8. Paul was stoned at _____.

9. John had been banished to the Isle of
   _____.

10. Luke portrayed Christ as the _____ of
    publicans and sinners.

Apply Your Knowledge

Many professing Christians of our day have become egocentric or self-centered. This seems a far cry from the thinking of the first century church. How can you account for the sacrificial living and powerful witness of those early believers? Try to apply the principles that were so evident in that earlier day to your life today.

Expand Your Knowledge

Since the early church was such a powerful force that it shook the world, we should be able to learn much from a study of the Book of Acts. Consider such a study using the following resources available from the Pentecostal Publishing House.

Books
- *Acts* by Jet Witherspoon Toole
- *Acts: God's Training Manual for Today's Church* by James Poitras (three volumes)
- *Salvation in the Book of Acts* by Fred Kinzie

CD
- *Acts of the Apostles* by Arlo Moehlenpah
  (PowerPoint presentations plus Microsoft Word documents of handouts, quizzes, and more)

The Pentecostal Experience Through the Ages

*And I say also unto thee, That thou art Peter,
and upon this rock I will build my church; and
the gates of hell shall not prevail against it.*

Matthew 16:18

Start with the Scriptures

I Kings 19:9-18   Revelation 2:12-29; 3:1-6
Malachi 3:15-18

The Principle and Promise
of Preservation

God's truth endures to all generations (Psalm 100:5). God has always had a people; even in times of great apostasy, He has had a remnant who believed and obeyed Him.

In Romans 11, the apostle Paul derived an important principle from the story of Elijah—the principle of preservation. That is, God always has a remnant. Even when His people as a whole reject Him, some still serve Him according to the truth.

When Jesus Christ told the apostles of His plan to establish the New Testament church, He assured them that the gates of hell would not stand against that church (Matthew 16:18). This statement indicates that the Lord will always have disciples who are victorious over the forces of evil and that Satan will never be able to wipe the church out of existence. In other words, Jesus gave His church the promise of preservation.

In Revelation 2 and 3, the Lord sent letters to seven churches in Asia Minor. They were actual churches in the first century, but their circumstances and conditions are relevant in every age, including today. Jesus praised two of them, rebuked one, and both praised and rebuked the other four. Significantly, in each letter He promised a reward to the overcomer, indicating that in every case some people would be victorious over sin. Regarding one of the weakest churches, He stated, "Thou hast a few names even in Sardis which have not defiled their garments" (Revelation 3:4).

Based on these scriptural passages, we believe that the New Testament church, as defined by the apostles' doctrine and experience, has existed in every age since the Day of Pentecost. In this chapter we will examine the historical record to see what evidence exists to support this conclusion.

The Record of Preservation

At the outset of our survey, we must note several difficulties in attempting such a study of history.

Adequate records are not always available. Religious leaders often destroyed writings they judged unorthodox and suppressed views they considered false, dangerous, or unimportant. Other historical information may have been lost or over-looked by historians. Even today, it is often difficult to find information about Oneness Pentecostalism in libraries, despite the size of this movement and the lack of suppression of publications in the western world.

Records that do exist are often slanted in favor of majority doctrinal views. This occurs either intentionally or unintentionally, for history is written by the victors.

Many ancient writings contain changes or additions made by copyists over the centuries. This happened often for doctrinal reasons.

Existing documents do not always reflect the views of the average believer of the time. Instead, they reflect the view of an unrepresentative elite.

False doctrines existed from the earliest times. Many New Testament examples, warnings, and predictions show this to be so, so the antiquity of a belief or writing is no guarantee of doctrinal accuracy.

With these cautions in mind, let us investigate certain distinctives of apostolic Christianity that Christendom today generally does not accept. In particular, we will examine the new birth experience of Acts 2 (repentance, baptism in Jesus' name, and the baptism of the Holy Spirit) and the doctrine of Oneness (the absolute oneness of God and the absolute deity of Jesus Christ, in contrast to trinitarianism). Chapter 1 discussed the Pentecostal outpouring of the first century, and chapter 3 discusses the great Pentecostal revival of the twentieth century; this chapter explores the intervening period.

The Oneness of God

Second century. The first generation of Christian writers after the apostles are commonly known as the Apostolic Fathers, or more accurately, the Post-Apostolic Fathers. They wrote around AD 90-140, and the most prominent of them were Ignatius, Clement of Rome, and Polycarp. They adhered closely to biblical language and thought, affirming strict monotheism, the absolute deity of Jesus Christ, and the true humanity of Christ. They did not use distinctive trinitarian terms, and their writings are compatible with the Oneness message.

The New Catholic Encyclopedia says concerning trinitarianism in the second century, "Among the Apostolic Fathers, there had been nothing even remotely approaching such a mentality or perspective; among the second century Apologists, little more than a focusing of the problem as that of plurality within the Godhead. . . . A trinitarian solution was still in the future."

Third century. Tertullian, who is often called the father of trinitarianism, was the first writer to speak of God as a "trinity" and as "three persons." Nevertheless, comments by early trinitarians reveal that well into the third century the majority of believers still adhered to the biblical doctrine of Oneness.

Novatian acknowledged that "very many heretics" accept Jesus as the Father. Hippolytus wrote that "no one is ignorant" of this belief. Origen acknowledged that "some individuals among the multitude of believers . . . incautiously assert that the Savior is the Most High God." Most significantly, Tertullian admitted that "the majority of believers" were opposed to his doctrine of the trinity, seeing it as a compromise of monotheism and of their historic confession of faith.

Historians call the people of this time who opposed trinitarianism, affirmed God's oneness, and affirmed the absolute deity of Jesus Christ "modalists" or "modalistic monarchians." *Encyclopedia Britannica* defines their belief as follows:

"Modalistic monarchianism, conceiving that the whole fulness of the Godhead dwelt in Christ . . . maintained that the names Father and Son were only different designations of the same subject, the one God, who 'with reference to the relations in which He had previously stood to the world is called the Father, but in reference to His appearance in humanity is called the Son.'"

The most prominent modalist leaders were Noetus of Smyrna, Praxeas, and Sabellius. Noetus was Praxeas's teacher in Asia Minor, Praxeas preached in Rome about 190, and Sabellius preached in Rome about 215. Since Sabellius was the best known, historians often call the doctrine Sabellianism.

Sabellius relied heavily upon Scripture, especially passages such as Exodus 20:3, Deuteronomy 6:4, Isaiah 44:6, John 10:30, and John 10:38. None of the writings of the modalists survive; we get our information about them from their doctrinal opponents. From the sparse evidence we have, it appears that they embraced the central beliefs of Oneness.

Other modalists were Epigonus, Cleomenes, some of the Montanists, and apparently the Roman bishops Callistus and Zephyrinus, whom the Roman Catholic Church classifies as popes.

Fourth century. In addition to the followers of Sabellius, people of this time who are usually classified as modalists were Marcellus of Ancyra, Photinus, Commodian, and Priscillian.

Medieval era. Modalists of this time were the Sabellians, the Priscillianists, and possibly unknown "heretics." Numerous people in this age questioned the doctrine of the trinity, but it is not always clear what their precise beliefs were.

Sixteenth to eighteenth centuries. Here is a list of some prominent people who affirmed the deity of Jesus Christ while either denying trinitarianism or expressing serious doubts about it: Michael

Servetus (whose doctrine was known to Luther, Zwingli, and Calvin and who was burned at the stake with Calvin's approval), Emmanuel Swedenborg (who recognized the error of trinitarianism but taught some unusual, nonbiblical doctrines), some Anabaptists, many antitrinitarians, William Penn and many early Quakers, Isaac Watts, Isaac Newton.

Nineteenth century. Writers of this century who expressed Oneness views were John Cloves (England), John Miller (U.S.), and some New England Congregationalists.

Repentance

All branches of Christendom acknowledge the necessity of repentance, at least in theory. The early post-apostolic church emphasized repentance strongly and demanded evidence of repentance before water baptism. There was such insistence on a total life transformation that some taught no forgiveness was available for major sins committed after baptism. The gradual shift to infant baptism did away with true repentance, however, until in the Roman Catholic Church repentance evolved into penance and salvation by works.

The Protestant Reformers rejected this distortion, but because of their emphasis on mental faith alone and predestination, they did not completely restore the biblical doctrine of repentance. They held that repentance precedes the moment of faith or is equivalent to the moment of faith. As a result, most evangelicals today emphasize an instant mental decision for Christ, typically consisting of a simple gesture, a repeated prayer, or a silent thought. Unfortunately, this action is not necessarily accompanied by godly sorrow, a decision to forsake sin, or a transformed life.

Water Baptism

For the first five centuries, water baptism was universally accepted as an initiation rite performed for the washing away of sins and therefore essential to salvation. Eventually, however, it came to be viewed as a magical ceremony instead of an act of faith. Catholics, Orthodox, many Lutherans, some Protestant scholars, and the Churches of Christ teach it to be part of salvation. Luther, the *Augsburg Confession* (an early Lutheran creed), and the *Lutheran Catechism* all stated that baptism is necessary to salvation, made effective by faith. Most Protestants today see it as symbolic only, however.

Most of Christendom uses the trinitarian baptismal formula, except for Oneness Pentecostals and many charismatics. But a study of church history reveals that the original formula was Jesus Name and that the early post-apostolic church used the name of Jesus in the baptismal formula. So concludes the *Encyclopedia of Religion and Ethics* and the *Interpreter's Dictionary of the Bible*, as well as church historians Otto Heick, Williston Walker, Jean Danielou, Wilhelm Bousset, and many others. Most of the people we have identified as expressing Oneness beliefs apparently baptized in Jesus' name also.

Second century. The Post-Apostolic Fathers made no reference to a trinitarian baptismal formula, but they attached great significance to the name of God in salvation, and it appears that they followed the apostles' practice of baptizing in Jesus' name.

Herman wrote of baptism "in the name of the Lord" and in the "name of the Son of God." Irenaeus stated, "We are made clean, by means of the sacred water and the invocation of the Lord." The heretic Marcion broke away from the church during this time, and his followers preserved the older baptism "in the name of Jesus Christ." The *Acts of Paul and Thecla*, written by an Asiatic presbyter, gives an account of baptism "in the name of Jesus Christ."

A document called the *Didache* speaks both of baptism "into the name of the Lord" and baptism "into the name of the Father and of the Son and of the Holy Ghost." It does not otherwise allude to the trinity, however, and the latter phrase could easily be a later insertion, for the only existing Greek manuscript dates from 1056.

Most scholars assert that Justin Martyr was the first to mention a threefold formula, around 150. He did not recite the modern formula but explicitly included the name Jesus, apparently in deference to older practice: "in the name of God, the Father and Lord of the universe, and of our Saviour Jesus Christ and of the Holy Spirit." It seems that this formula was a transitional step to the later trinitarian formula. Similarly, Justin's view of Jesus as a subordinate second person of the Godhead was a transition from original monotheism to later trinitarianism.

Third century. Stephen, bishop of Rome, held Jesus Name baptism to be valid. Cyprian denounced "heretics" in his day who "baptized in the name of Jesus Christ" instead of "in the full and united Trinity."

A Treatise on Rebaptism by an Anonymous Writer, probably written by a bishop who opposed Cyprian, makes a strong case for the validity of Jesus Name baptism even when performed by people outside the recognized church. It says that such people do not need to be rebaptized: "Heretics who are already baptized in water in the name of Jesus Christ must only be baptized with the Holy Spirit." Moreover, this position had the support of "the most ancient custom and ecclesiastical tradition" and "the authority of so many years, and so many churches and apostles and bishops." Not only were "heretics" baptized by "invoking the name of the Lord Jesus," but many people, both "Jews and Gentiles, fully believing as they ought, are in like manner baptized."

Fourth century. Ambrose, although a trinitarian, held that baptism in Jesus' name was valid. But the Council of Constantinople in 381 condemned "Sabellian baptism," which it described as prevalent in Galatia.

Middle ages. Numerous condemnations of Sabellian baptism during this time indicate that some people kept the issue alive. For example, the church in Constantinople condemned Sabellian baptism in a letter to Antioch around 450, the Justinian Code of 529 (Byzantine Empire) declared the death penalty for both antitrinitarianism and rebaptism, the Council of Constantinople in 553 again condemned Sabellian baptism, and Martin Damiun (died 579), bishop of Braga, condemned "single immersion under a single name."

Nevertheless, Bede of England (673-735) accepted the validity of baptism in Jesus' name, as did the Council of Frejus (792) and Pope Nicholas I (858-67). Other medieval writers who mentioned the Jesus Name formula were Peter Lombard, Hugo Victor, and Thomas Aquinas.

Sixteenth to nineteenth centuries. Martin Luther encountered a dispute over the Jesus Name formula in his day. Many antitrinitarians began to baptize in Jesus' name. For example, in 1572 George Schomann was baptized in "the name of Christ."

Thomas Edwards of England wrote in 1646 about some "heretics" who taught that trinitarian baptism was a man-made tradition and that Christian baptism was "only in the name of Jesus Christ." An English Baptist document dated 1660 endorsed the formula of "in the name of the Lord Jesus Christ," citing Acts 2:38.

Many of the Plymouth Brethren, as well as some other English groups, taught on the authority of Acts 2:38 that baptism should be in the name of Jesus only. John Miller, a Presbyterian minister in the United States, interpreted Matthew 28:19 to refer to baptism in Jesus' name as described in the Book of Acts.

The Baptism of the Holy Spirit

In theory, all major branches of Christendom teach that the baptism of the Holy Spirit is necessary to salvation. Catholics, Orthodox, and Protestants all teach that they receive the Holy Spirit. They do not usually recognize speaking in tongues as the initial evidence of the Holy Spirit, however. Most Holiness people, trinitarian Pentecostals, and charismatics teach that the baptism of the Holy Spirit is an optional, postconversional extra blessing.

Second century. The Post-Apostolic Fathers spoke of the outpouring of the Holy Spirit and of the exercise of spiritual gifts. The *Didache* and Justin Martyr also mentioned with approval the gifts of the Spirit, including prophecy. Irenaeus specifically testified to the existence of speaking in tongues, describing it as the sign of a Spirit-filled person. Celsus, a pagan, stated that Christians in his day spoke in tongues. A group called the Montanists emphasized the Holy Spirit and spoke in tongues.

Third century. Tertullian identified speaking in tongues as one of the marks of a true church. Novatian cited with approval the existence of tongues and other spiritual gifts in the church. Based on passages in Epiphanius and Pseudo-Athanasius, it appears that Sabellius received the Holy Spirit and spoke in tongues.

Fourth and fifth centuries. Hilary and Ambrose taught in favor of tongues, but a little later, Augustine opposed "heretics" who still taught that people spoke in tongues at conversion. Both Augustine and John Chrysostom admitted that in former times everyone who received the Holy Spirit spoke in tongues, but they argued (wrongly) that tongues had now ceased.

Middle ages. Speaking in tongues was reported among "heretics" such as the Waldenses and Albigenses, and also among the Franciscans and other mendicant orders of monks.

Sixteenth century. Some Anabaptists spoke in tongues, as did people in a prophecy movement in England. Menno Simons, the Anabaptist leader whose followers became known as Mennonites, described speaking in tongues as expected evidence of the Holy Ghost, and many early Anabaptists worshiped quite demonstratively.

Seventeenth century. Speaking in tongues occurred among the Camisards in southern France, the early Quakers in England, the Jansenists (a Catholic reform movement) in France, and the Pietists (including Moravians) in Germany.

Eighteenth century. Speaking in tongues continued in some of these groups and was also reported among the Methodists in England and America. John Wesley, founder of the Methodists, heard of speaking in tongues and defended it as a valid Christian experience for his day. The Wesleyan revivals were noted for physical demonstrations in repentance and worship.

Nineteenth century. Reports of speaking in tongues grew more numerous, coming from among (1) American revivals and camp meetings conducted by Methodists, Baptists, and some Presbyterians; (2) Lutheran followers of Gustav von Below in Germany; (3) Irvingites in England and America;

(4) Plymouth Brethren in England; (5) Readers (Lasare) in Sweden; (6) revivals in Ireland; and (7) Holiness people in America, particularly in Tennessee and North Carolina.

Conclusion

We do not necessarily agree with all the doctrines of every individual or movement discussed in this lesson, but our investigation has demonstrated a basic truth: through the ages people have believed, preached, and experienced repentance, baptism in Jesus' name, and the baptism of the Holy Spirit with the sign of tongues. These doctrines are not modern-day inventions; the Bible teaches them, and many throughout history have practiced them.

In particular, it can be stated that some groups adhered simultaneously to baptism in Jesus' name and the baptism of the Spirit with tongues. The Book of Acts and the Epistles show that the first-century apostolic church adhered to them. We also find them practiced by the early post-apostolic church (second century), the early Sabellians (third century), and modern Pentecostals and charismatics (twentieth century). The historical evidence also indicates that both doctrines existed among Montanists (second and third centuries), later Sabellians (fourth, fifth, and sixth centuries), various "heretics" (third and fourth centuries and Middle Ages), Anabaptists (sixteenth century), antitrinitarians (sixteenth and seventeenth centuries), early Quakers (seventeenth century), and Plymouth Brethren (nineteenth century). Satan has evidently tried to suppress the facts, but there is enough evidence to indicate that the apostolic church has existed since the Day of Pentecost.

Test Your Knowledge

1. Why is it sometimes difficult to find historical records of the Pentecostal experience?

2. What terms do historians use for Christians of early centuries who opposed trinitarianism while affirming the absolute deity of Jesus Christ?

3. Name some groups since 1500 in which speaking in tongues was reported.

4. Is there any evidence that both baptism in Jesus' name and receiving the Holy Spirit with tongues occurred among the same groups of people? If so, which groups?

5. In order to believe and teach the Pentecostal experience, is it necessary to prove from historical records that it existed in every age? Why or why not?

Apply Your Knowledge

History itself can never prove the validity of doctrine, for the Bible is our sole authority. But history can provide insight into how key doctrines were altered or lost over the centuries, and it can help dispel the myth that these doctrines are of recent origin.

Expand Your Knowledge

For further information, see *The Oneness of God*; *History of Christian Doctrine, Vols. I, II and III*; and *The New Birth* by David K. Bernard. Another helpful book is *Ancient Champions of Oneness* by William Chalfant. Several compilations of ancient church writings are available; the most comprehensive is *The AnteNicene Fathers*, a ten-volume set. Helpful general reference works are *Encyclopedia of Religion and Ethics*, *Encyclopedia Britannica*, and *The New Schaff-Herzog Encyclopedia of Religious Knowledge*.

3

The Twentieth-Century Pentecostal Revival

With all lowliness and meekness, with long-suffering, forbearing one another in love; endeavouring to keep the unity of the Spirit in the bond of peace.

Ephesians 4:2-3

Start with the Scriptures

Psalm 133:1
Ephesians 4:1-6, 11-16

Colossians 3:12-17

In December 1900, Charles Fox Parham, the founder and leader of Bethel Bible College, asked the approximately forty students to search the Bible to determine the sign or evidence that occurs when a person receives the Holy Ghost. After three days, the students assembled with their answer: the initial evidence of receiving the Holy Ghost is speaking with other languages as the Spirit gives the utterance.

Parham was surprised by the answer, and he was also surprised when on January 1, 1901, one student,

Agnes N. Ozman, began speaking with tongues when he laid hands on her in prayer. Two days later, on January 3, 1901, Parham found twelve other students, including his wife, praying and speaking with tongues. Parham, sensing a holy presence, knelt in prayer and soon received the Holy Ghost with the evidence of speaking with tongues.

During the next few weeks, the experience spread among the other students and into the community. On January 21, Parham and some of the students held their first public evangelistic service in Kansas City. Newspapers in Topeka and Kansas City reported on the "new sect," with front page coverage in Kansas City.

Revival in Texas

In the spring of 1905, Parham held a meeting in Orchard, Texas, a small community about forty miles west of Houston. Parham stated that before he arrived only a few people in Orchard professed to be Christians, but before the meeting ended almost the entire community was converted. In July Parham moved his group of workers into Houston, holding meetings in the Brunner Holiness Church and in Bryant Hall. W. F. Carothers, the pastor of Brunner Holiness Church, accepted the Pentecostal experience as did his congregation.

In the fall of 1905, Parham opened a short-term Bible school in the downtown area of Houston. About twenty-five workers from Kansas came to help him in Texas, most of whom attended the Bible school. Howard Goss was among these workers.

Azusa Street Mission

One student who attended the Bible school in Houston, William J. Seymour, a black Holiness minister living in Houston, went to Los Angeles,

California, to preach in a Holiness church on Santa Fe Street. Although Seymour had not received the Holy Ghost, his sermon on the first Sunday morning, February 24, was taken from Acts 2:4. He preached that the initial sign of receiving the Holy Ghost is speaking with tongues.

The pastor, Julia Hutchins, did not agree with his doctrine, so she locked the door to keep him from preaching in the church. A family from the church, however, invited Seymour to stay at their house, and another family opened their home on Bonnie Brae Street for prayer meetings.

On April 9, Jeannie Moore, a young lady who later married Seymour, and several other people received the Holy Ghost during the prayer meeting. Three days later, on April 12, Seymour was filled with the Holy Ghost. On April 15, Miss Moore gave her testimony at a local church; and soon large crowds filled the house and overflowed into the yard and street.

By April 18, the group moved to an old two-story building on Azusa Street in the downtown industrial area of Los Angeles. By the end of that summer, hundreds of people had been filled with the Spirit, and the Azusa Street revival was ready to spread across North America and around the world.

Holiness ministers who came to the Azusa Street Mission to receive the Holy Ghost returned to proclaim the Pentecostal experience to their churches, cities, and communities. Many church congregations and several entire Holiness organizations came into the Pentecostal movement. Pentecostals became missionaries to Africa, India, China, the Mideast, South America, and Europe. Several missionaries from other church organizations visited Azusa Street to receive the Holy Ghost, and they took the news back to their fields of ministry.

Early Pentecostal Leadership

From 1901 to 1907, the Pentecostal movement, known at the time as the Apostolic Faith Movement, was led in a general way by Parham. Seymour was the recognized leader of the Azusa Street Mission in Los Angeles, and for a brief moment he enjoyed widespread influence. One of the earliest leaders whose influence continued for several decades was Howard A. Goss.

After Goss received the Holy Ghost in the spring of 1906, Parham appointed him to be the field supervisor of the work in Texas. Parham also appointed W. F. Carothers to be the general field supervisor, and Carothers signed Goss's first ministerial license, issued on August 26, 1906. Parham's effort to organize the Pentecostal movement in Texas crumbled in 1907.

Goss, however, remained a leader among the Pentecostals in Texas, Oklahoma, Arkansas, Kansas, Missouri, and other midwestern states. During the years from 1907 to 1914, he established Pentecostal churches in Texas and Arkansas, and he evangelized in Texas, Arkansas, Missouri, Kansas, Illinois, and Iowa. He met William H. Durham and preached at the church he pastored in Chicago. In 1908, he met E. N. Bell, to whom he turned the pastorate of the large church he had pioneered in Malvern, Arkansas. He also turned the paper he edited, *The Apostolic Faith*, to Bell, who merged it with the *Word and Witness* in 1910.

Goss was the prime individual behind the organization of the Assemblies of God in 1914. Earlier, in 1910, he worked out a temporary arrangement with C. H. Mason to obtain and issue license in the name of the black organization Mason founded, the Church of God in Christ. In 1912, Goss became acquainted with H. G. Rodgers and his group in Alabama and solicited his support. In late 1913, he persuaded Bell, D. C. O. Opperman, and others to sponsor a call for an organizing conference of interested Pentecostal ministers. The conference, meeting in Hot Springs, Arkansas, where Goss was the host pastor, formed the Assemblies of God. Goss, Bell, and Opperman were among those chosen to be top officials in the new organization.

Doctrinal Issues

The first doctrinal division in the Pentecostal movement came from the teachings of William H. Durham. Although Durham earlier embraced the Holiness doctrine on sanctification, soon after he received the Holy Ghost he began preaching that sanctification is not a second work of grace but is accomplished at the time of conversion and continues to move a person toward perfection throughout his Christian life. By 1912, his doctrine, which became known as "The Finished Work of Calvary," had been accepted by most of the independent Pentecostal ministers.

The second doctrinal issue to divide the Pentecostal movement had its beginnings in 1913 during the Arroyo Seco camp meeting held near Los Angeles. Ministering at a baptismal service, R. E. McAlister noted that the church in the Book of Acts always baptized in the name of Jesus Christ and not in the traditional formula of "the name of the Father, and of the Son, and of the Holy Ghost." His observation immediately stirred interest.

One minister, Frank J. Ewart, studied the Bible for several months in search for the answer to the supposed conflict between Jesus' command in Matthew 28:19 and the formula used by the church in the Book of Acts. By the spring of 1914, Ewart had reached the conclusion that the singular name in Matthew 28:19 was Jesus Christ. To support this view he pointed to the baptismal accounts in Acts and to the references in the Epistles, but he also noted the full deity of Jesus Christ: "For in him dwelleth all the fulness of the Godhead bodily" (Colossians 2:9).

Ewart explained his understanding of baptism in the name of Jesus Christ to several other Pentecostal ministers. Some rejected his teaching but others enthusiastically embraced it. On April 15, 1914, Ewart rebaptized Glenn Cook in the name of Jesus Christ, and Cook rebaptized him. This decision to rebaptize Pentecostals set in motion an issue that soon divided the Pentecostal movement between the trinitarians and the Jesus Name believers.

After Cook's successful preaching tour of the Midwest, several leaders of the newly organized Assemblies of God, including Goss, Bell, and J. R. Flower, denounced the "new issue." Writing in the *Word and Witness* in the July 17, 1915, issue, Flower stated his opinion that the matter was only a fad and would soon fade away on its own.

An event that shocked the trinitarians was Bell's baptism in the name of Jesus Christ during a camp meeting in Jackson, Tennessee, in August 1915. Joining him were many other ministers, including H. G. Rodgers, and hundreds of laymen. Later that same summer, Bell baptized Goss at a camp meeting in Arkansas.

By the time the General Council convened in St. Louis in October 1915, it appeared that the Assemblies of God organization would embrace water baptism in the name of Jesus Christ. A list of prominent Pentecostal leaders who had accepted Jesus Name baptism included not only Bell, Goss, Ewart, Cook, Roberts, Haywood, and Rodgers, but also R. E. McAlister, D. C. O. Opperman, George T. Studd, Harvey Shearer, L. C. Hall, B. F. Lawrence,

Harry Van Loon, Frank Small, A. H. Argue, W. E. Booth-Clibborn, R. J. Scott, Elmer K. Fisher, and Robert L. LaFleur.

The "new issue" was debated at the General Council with E. N. Bell and G. T. Haywood presenting the case for water baptism in the name of Jesus Christ, and A. P. Collins and Jacob Miller presenting the traditional formula, "in the name of the Father, and of the Son, and of the Holy Ghost." The issue was not settled at the Council, but the ministers agreed to pray and to study the matter during the coming year.

By the time the General Council convened in St. Louis in October 1916, the trinitarian majority had organized to force the Oneness ministers to accept the trinitarian formula or to leave the organization. A committee of trinitarians, appointed by the trinitarian leadership, drew up a "Statement of Fundamental Truths" and presented it to the Council. The Statement embraced the trinitarian formula and made the doctrine of the trinity a basis for membership.

Between sixty and eighty ministers attended the General Council, of whom about fifteen or twenty were committed to the Oneness message. Many others were undecided or sympathetic toward the Oneness view, but most of them voted with the trinitarian majority in favor of the Statement.

The adoption of the Statement of Fundamental Truths forced the withdrawal of about one fourth of the ministers from the Council. After the General Council in 1916, the list of ordained ministers in the Assemblies of God fell from 585 to 429.

The Oneness Ministers Organize

In January 1917, a group of Oneness Pentecostal ministers met in St. Louis to form the General Assembly of the Apostolic Assemblies. The officers chosen were: D. C. O. Opperman, general chairman; Lee Floyd, secretary; Howard Goss, credential committee; and H. G. Rodgers, member of credential committee. This organization lasted only one year, however, since the government would not grant military exemption or railroad discount fares to the ministers in the young organization.

In January 1918, the General Assembly of the Apostolic Assemblies merged with the Pentecostal Assemblies of the World (P.A.W.), a Pentecostal organization that apparently began in Los Angeles in 1907. The merger reorganized the P.A.W. with new officers: J. J. Frazee, general chairman; D. C. O. Opperman, secretary; Howard Goss, treasurer. By its next conference in October 1918, Edward W. Doak had become general chairman, and W. E. Booth-Clibborn had become the secretary. In January 1919, the headquarters of the P.A.W. was moved from Portland, Oregon, to Indianapolis, Indiana, and the organization was incorporated in the state of Indiana. E. W. Doak remained as general overseer and G. T. Haywood became the general secretary.

For the first few years, this racially integrated organization functioned smoothly, but by 1921 racial tension was felt and exhibited. In this year a Southern Bible Conference of white ministers was held in Little Rock, Arkansas. This conference had an emotional impact on those in attendance, and it became the seed of the later split in the organization.

Division and Mergers

In spite of efforts by leaders of both races to maintain unity, misunderstanding continued to grow until in the fall of 1924 a division came on racial lines. Most of the white ministers withdrew to create a white organization, but by the end of 1925 they had created three white organizations.

In February 1925, a group of white ministers met in Jackson, Tennessee, to form the Pentecostal Ministerial Alliance (P.M.A.). They chose L. C. Hall as general chairman and Howard Goss as secretary-treasurer. Later, in 1932, the name of this organization was changed to Pentecostal Church Incorporated.

Many of the white ministers who felt that the P.M.A. was only a ministerial organization and that it did not properly recognize churches met in Houston, Texas, in October to organize the Emmanuel's Church in Jesus Christ (E.C. in J.C.), with W. T. Lyons as chairman and G. C. Stroud as secretary. O. F. Fauss was the third member of the board.

Between February and November of this same year, a third group organized under the name of the Apostolic Church of Jesus Christ (A.C. of J.C.), under the leadership of W. H. Whittington, with headquarters in St. Louis, Missouri. This group held its first conference to draw up a statement of doctrine during April 1926.

Most of the ministers were not satisfied to have organizational divisions among the Oneness Pentecostals. From the outset, leaders sought to bring the groups together again in one organization. Many attempts failed, but successes also came. The first merger occurred in 1928 when the Emmanuel's Church in Jesus Christ merged with the Apostolic Church of Jesus Christ, using the latter's name. O. F. Fauss was chosen as chairman, W. H. Whittington as secretary, and E. D. Browning as treasurer.

The next merger took place in 1932. The Apostolic Church of Jesus Christ merged with the Pentecostal Assemblies of the World, creating a racially integrated organization once again. The new organization took its name, the Pentecostal Assemblies of Jesus Christ, from the names of the two former organizations. This merger was not accepted by all the black ministers, however, and they continued the charter of the P.A.W.

This second attempt to integrate the races eventually failed for the same reasons the first attempt failed, racial prejudice in society and by both races. When the white majority voted to hold the General Conference in Tulsa, Oklahoma, in 1937, many of the black ministers felt that the whites had violated the merger agreement, and most of them soon drifted back to the P.A.W.

The United Pentecostal Church

From our point in history, the most important merger took place in 1945 when the Pentecostal Assemblies of Jesus Christ merged with the Pentecostal Church Incorporated to form the United Pentecostal Church. The word *international* was added December 14, 1972.

In the spring of 1945, a committee composed of members from both organizations met twice in St. Louis to work toward an agreement for the merger. The leaders carefully explored various potential problems and found acceptable solutions. The most difficult question had to do with the new birth. While most Oneness ministers identified the new birth with Acts 2:38, others did not take such a firm view.

The solution came when W. T. Witherspoon retired to a private room where he wrote the Fundamental Doctrine Statement that was readily accepted by all. The statement reads: "The basic and fundamental doctrine of this organization shall be the Bible standard of full salvation, which is repentance, baptism in water by immersion in the name of the Lord Jesus Christ, and the baptism of the Holy Ghost with the initial sign of speaking with other tongues as the Spirit gives utterance. We shall endeavor to keep the unity of the Spirit until we all come into the unity of the faith; at the same time admonishing all brethren that they shall not contend for their different views to the disunity of the body."

At the merger conference, the following officers were elected: Howard Goss as the general superintendent; W. T. Witherspoon as the assistant general superintendent; Stanley W. Chambers as the secretary-treasurer; T. R. Dungan as assistant secretary-treasurer; and Wynn T. Stairs as Foreign Missions secretary. Brother M. J. Wolff became the editor of the *Pentecostal Herald*, the official organ of the organization. The united organization had 1,833 ministers and from 700 to 900 churches.

In the year 2007 the United Pentecostal Church International reported more than 4,143 churches and over 9,121 ministers in the United States and Canada, with an approximate Sunday attendance of 550,000; it is estimated that the constituency of the United Pentecostal Church in North America exceeds 800,000. Missionary work is promoted in more than 177 nations with a foreign constituency of nearly 1.7 million.

Test Your Knowledge

1. In what year did the Pentecostal revival of this century begin?

2. What is the significance of the Azusa Street revival?

3. In what year was the Assemblies of God organized?

4. In what year and in what camp meeting was baptism in the name of Jesus first mentioned?

5. Name some of the Pentecostal leaders who were baptized in the name of Jesus Christ.

6. In what year did the trinitarians force the Oneness ministers out of the Assemblies of God?

7. What was the first racially integrated Oneness organization? Why did division come?

8. What three white organizations were formed in 1925?

9. In what year was the United Pentecostal Church formed?

10. What is the fundamental doctrine of the United Pentecostal Church?

Apply Your Knowledge

Write a history of the local church. You may find the events and people to be enlightening and inspiring. Your work will also help others to understand the dedication and commitment of those who pioneered the church.

Expand Your Knowledge

Two informative books on the history of the United Pentecostal Church are *United We Stand* by Arthur L. Clanton and *Twentieth-Century Pentecostals* by Fred J. Foster. Two other resource books are *Our God Is One, the Story of the Oneness Pentecostals* by Talmadge L. French and *History of Christian Doctrine, Volume III*, by David K. Bernard. An excellent reference book on Pentecostals in general is *Dictionary of Pentecostal and Charismatic Movements* edited by Stanley Burgess and Gary McGee. Biographies include *What God Hath Wrought* by O. F. Fauss, *The Winds of God* by Ethel Goss, and *The Phenomenon of Pentecost* by Frank Ewart. Other historical books include *The Life of Andrew Bar-David Urshan*, an autobiography; *Pentecostal Pioneer Women, Volumes I and II*; and *Profiles of Pentecostal Preachers, Volumes I and II*, compiled by Mary Wallace.

4

The True Faith

Holding fast the faithful word as he hath been taught, that he may be able by sound doctrine both to exhort and to convince the gainsayers.

Titus 1:9

Start with the Scriptures

Matthew 28:19
John 1:9
Galatians 1:8

Ephesians 4:11
I Timothy 4:1
Revelation 22:18-19

True and False Doctrine

Some Christians are hesitant to speak of doctrine, for it seems to them to imply sectarianism. Some have even gone so far as to say that doctrine is unimportant. But the word *doctrine* simply means "teaching." And the practice of Christianity cannot be accomplished apart from teaching.

Jesus said, "Go ye therefore, and teach all nations" (Matthew 28:19).

It is God Himself who has placed teachers in the church (I Corinthians 12:28; Ephesians 4:11). A teacher, by definition, imparts doctrine.

There is such a thing as true doctrine; that is, teaching which is faithful to the Scriptures (I Timothy 4:16; II Timothy 3:15-16). And there is false doctrine, or teaching that is not faithful to the Scriptures (I Timothy 4:1; II Peter 3:16).

Sources of Doctrine

It is obvious that there are many conflicting doctrines taught in Christendom today. How can this be since all claim to be right? One of the basic reasons for doctrinal variation is differing opinions as to legitimate sources of doctrine.

Tradition. Some denominations teach that church tradition is a legitimate source of doctrine. That is, if it can be proven that the church has held to a certain teaching for centuries, and especially if that teaching has the authority of a church council or creed, it is accepted as true.

Religious scholars admit that the doctrine of the trinity is not found in the Bible, but many church organizations accept this doctrine as true on the claim that it has the tradition of the church behind it. (See Edmund J. Fortman, *The Triune God—A Historical Study of the Doctrine of the Trinity* [Grand Rapids, MI: Baker Book House, 1972].)

Since the Bible declares that we must teach "sound doctrine" (Titus 2:1) and that true doctrine is necessary to salvation (I Timothy 4:16), we cannot be content with doctrine that has no scriptural authority. Every tradition must be examined by the Word of God to determine the accuracy or error of the tradition.

Private revelation. Some religious movements embrace "revelations" received by their founders. In these cases the "revelations" are thought to be at least equal to or even exceed the authority of Scripture.

These "revelations" take on various forms, but usually they include a "prophet" who claims to have divine knowledge beyond the Bible.

The danger of doctrine based on private revelation should be evident: At some point, all of these "revelations" contradict, add to, or apply false meanings to the inspired Word of God. Scriptures are then ignored in favor of the doctrine of the "prophet."

Scripture. The only trustworthy source of doctrine is the Bible, the Word of God.

The Preamble of the Articles of Faith of the United Pentecostal Church states: "The Bible is the only God-given authority which man possesses; therefore, all doctrine, faith, hope, and all instruction for the church must be based upon, and harmonize with, the Bible."

We have a strong and absolute commitment to teach as doctrine only what the Bible teaches. We are not interested in teaching more human tradition or extra-biblical revelations.

Jesus asked, "Why do ye also transgress the commandment of God by your tradition?" (Matthew 15:3). Christ also showed the vanity of human doctrines when He said, "But in vain they do worship me, teaching for doctrines the commandments of men" (Matthew 15:9).

On the subject of extra-biblical revelations, Paul said, "But though we, or an angel from heaven, preach any other gospel unto you than that which we have preached unto you, let him be accursed" (Galatians 1:8). Even angelic visitations are to be rejected if the angels proclaim something which contradicts the Word of God.

The seriousness of holding only to the Word of God for authority is seen in Revelation 22:18-19: "For I testify unto every man that heareth the words of the prophecy of this book, If any man shall add unto these things, God shall add unto him the plagues that are written in this book: And if any man shall take away from the words of the book of this prophecy, God shall take away his part out of the book of life, and out of the holy city, and from the things which are written in this book."

To the ancient Israelites, Moses said, "Ye shall not add unto the word which I command you, neither shall ye diminish ought from it, that ye may keep the commandments of the LORD your God which I command you" (Deuteronomy 4:2).

Later, Agur added, "Every word of God is pure: he is a shield unto them that put their trust in him. Add thou not unto his words, lest he reprove thee, and thou be found a liar" (Proverbs 30:5-6).

The only safe course of action for those who wish to please God is to reject all doctrines which appeal to any authority but the Scripture.

The Apostles' Doctrine

Concerning the church, Paul said it is "built upon the foundation of the apostles and prophets, Jesus Christ himself being the chief corner stone" (Ephesians 2:20). While Jesus Christ Himself is the basic foundation of the church (I Corinthians 3:11), the apostles and prophets are foundational in that they were the recipients of foundational revelation concerning the church (Ephesians 3:5-6). Therefore, the teaching of the apostles and prophets is fundamental to New Testament truth. To be sure that we are in the church as they were, we must carefully examine and follow their teaching.

The second chapter of the Book of Acts records the founding of the New Testament church. The apostle Peter preached the first message in the church, and it is recorded that "they that gladly received his word were baptized: and the same day there were added unto them about three thousand souls. And they continued stedfastly in the apostles' doctrine and fellowship, and in breaking of bread, and in prayers" (Acts 2:41-42).

The early church *continued stedfastly in the apostles' doctrine*. If the church today is to be true to the Word of God, it also must continue stedfastly in that same doctrine. It is for this reason that the United Pentecostal Church International is committed to adhering to the doctrine taught by the apostles and prophets of the New Testament.

The believers in the first century felt so strongly about the importance of true doctrine or teaching that they made uncompromising statements under the inspiration of the Holy Spirit:

- "If there come any unto you, and bring not this doctrine, receive him not into your house, neither bid him God speed" (II John 10).

- "A man that is an heretick after the first and second admonition reject; knowing that he that is such is subverted, and sinneth, being condemned of himself" (Titus 3:10-11).

- "For the time will come when they will not endure sound doctrine; but after their own lusts shall they heap to themselves teachers, having itching ears" (II Timothy 4:3).

- "Now I beseech you, brethren, mark them which cause divisions and offences contrary to the doctrine which ye have learned; and avoid them" (Romans 16:17).

- "And if any man obey not our word by this epistle, note that man, and have no company with him, that he may be ashamed" (II Thessalonians 3:14).

What are the doctrines taught by the early church? They are summarized in Hebrews 6:1-2: "Therefore leaving the principles of the doctrine of

48

Christ, let us go on unto perfection; not laying again the foundation of repentance from dead works, and of faith toward God, of the doctrine of baptisms, and of laying on of hands, and of resurrection of the dead, and of eternal judgment."

There are six elements of the doctrine of Christ:

- *Repentance*
- *Faith*
- *Baptisms*
- *Laying on of hands*
- *Resurrection of the dead*
- *Eternal judgment*

Repentance. The word *repent* comes from a Greek word which signifies "to have a change of heart, mind, and purpose." The person who repents of his dead works changes his mind about sin and about God. This change affects his way of living.

Repentance does not mean that a person will never sin again. He does not become infallible. But it does mean that he has changed the direction of his life. If he fails, he is to confess his sin to God and return to the right path.

Repentance is essential to salvation (Luke 13:3; Acts 17:30; II Peter 3:9). As a result, the message of repentance was on the lips of every New Testament preacher:

- *John the Baptist preached repentance* (Matthew 3:1-2).
- *Jesus preached repentance* (Matthew 4:17).
- *The twelve apostles preached repentance* (Luke 24:47).
- *Peter preached repentance* (Acts 2:38).
- *Paul preached repentance* (Acts 20:21).

Faith. Faith toward God is essential to salvation. The writer of Hebrews said, "Without faith it is impossible to please him" (Hebrews 11:6). Paul

49

declared, "For by grace are ye saved through faith" (Ephesians 2:8).

Jesus also declared the necessity of faith when He said, "He that believeth and is baptized shall be saved; but he that believeth not shall be damned" (Mark 16:16).

Many Scriptures support this clear biblical truth of salvation by faith in Jesus Christ. (See Acts 16:31; Romans 10:10; John 1:12.)

Genuine faith, however, is more than just mental agreement that something is true. It is not enough to mentally agree that Jesus lived, or even that He was indeed the Messiah. Genuine faith demonstrates itself by its actions—by obedience to God's Word. As James said, "Even so faith, if it hath not works, is dead, being alone" (James 2:17). (See also James 2:14, 18-26.) While a person is saved by grace through faith and not by works, if he really believes on Jesus Christ, he will obey His words.

Baptisms. It is significant that this principle of the doctrine of Christ is called the "doctrine of baptisms" rather than the doctrine of "baptism." The two baptisms that relate to salvation are water baptism and Spirit baptism.

Water baptism is an integral part of the Great Commission (Matthew 28:19). As we have already seen, Jesus listed both belief and baptism as essential to salvation (Mark 16:16).

It should be no surprise, then, that on the day of the birth of the church, the apostle Peter responded to the question from the crowd; "What shall we do?'' with these words: "Repent, and be baptized every one of you in the name of Jesus Christ for the remission of sins, and ye shall receive the gift of the Holy Ghost" (Acts 2:38).

There are many reasons that water baptism is to be administered in the name of Jesus Christ. Since water baptism is "for the remission of sins" and since the name of Jesus is the only name that saves from sin (Acts 4:12), it is needful for the name of Jesus to be spoken in water baptism. (See Matthew 1:21; Luke 24:47.)

Another reason water baptism is to be performed in the name of Jesus Christ is that baptism identifies the person with Christ (Romans 6:3-4). Moreover, baptism is the act of putting on Christ (Galatians 3:27). From the record in the Book of Acts and the epistles it is evident that the early church administered water baptism in the name of Jesus Christ (Acts 2:38; 8:16; 10:48; 19:5; 22:16; Romans 6:3-4; Galatians 3:27; Colossians 2:11-12).

Some have wondered if Peter's command to baptize in the name of Jesus Christ was a contradiction to Jesus' command to baptize in the name of the Father, and of the Son, and of the Holy Ghost (Matthew 28:19). But we should not suppose that the early church disobeyed the command of our Lord. Moreover, Peter had been given the keys to the kingdom by Jesus Himself (Matthew 16:19). We must assume that no contradiction exists between what Jesus said in Matthew 28:19 and what Peter said in Acts 2:38. Indeed, Peter's message must be viewed as fulfilling the command of Jesus.

Jesus said we are to baptize in the *name* (singular) of the Father, and of the Son, and of the Holy Ghost. We know that the name of the Son is Jesus (Matthew 1:21). The word "son" is not a name; it is a title showing relationship.

Neither is the word *father* a name. It is also a title of relationship. What is the name of the Father? Jesus said, "I am come in my Father's name" (John 5:43). Indeed, Jesus received His name by inheritance (Hebrews 1:4). Actually, the name "Jesus" is simply a transliteration of the Greek *Iesous*, which means "Jehovah-Savior."

The term "Holy Ghost" also forms a title. The word *ghost* simply means "spirit," while the word *holy* tells us the kind of spirit. In this case, it is the Spirit of God Himself. God is a Spirit (John 4:24). There is but one Spirit (Ephesians 4:4). We know that the Spirit of God would not have a name different from that of God Himself. This is borne out by the words of Jesus Himself: "But the Comforter, which is the Holy Ghost, whom the Father will send in my name . . ." (John 14:26). Just as Jesus came in His Father's name, so the Holy Spirit is identified with the name of Jesus.

There is, therefore, no disagreement between the command of Jesus in Matthew 28:19 and that of Peter in Acts 2:38. Both referred to the single name—Jesus—that is to be used in water baptism.

Another "baptism" in the doctrine of Christ is the baptism of the Holy Ghost. In his ministry as forerunner of Christ, John the Baptist predicted that Jesus would baptize with the Holy Ghost (Mark 1:8). During Jesus' last appearance to His disciples before His ascension, He commanded them not to leave Jerusalem until they were baptized with the Holy Ghost (Acts 1:4-8).

The Holy Spirit was given on the Day of Pentecost when the church was born (Acts 2:1-4). The gift or baptism of the Holy Ghost was the expected experience of all converts: Samaritans (Acts 8:14-17), Gentiles (Acts 10:44-48;11:15), and former followers of John the Baptist (Acts 19:1-6).

Peter said in his message on the first day of the church that those who repented and were baptized in the name of Jesus would "receive the gift of the Holy Ghost" (Acts 2:38). The universal nature of this promise is seen in the last part of his statement: "For the promise is unto you, and to your children, and to all that are afar off, even as many as the Lord our God shall call" (Acts 2:39).

It should be carefully noted that a sign from God Himself confirmed that the believers had received the Holy Ghost: they spoke in languages they had never learned, praising and glorifying God. This had been predicted by Jesus, who said, "And these signs shall follow them that believe . . . they shall speak with new tongues" (Mark 16:17). The word *tongues* means "languages." This was a clear sign that could not be mistaken. When the Holy Spirit caused a believer to speak in a language he did not know with his natural mind, it was the sign of the miracle of the new birth (Acts 2:4).

Today, just as in the New Testament, believers speak with new tongues when they receive the Holy Ghost and enter into the body of Christ.

Laying on of hands. Another principle of the doctrine of Christ is the laying on of hands. By this means, healing is ministered to the sick (Mark 16:18) and specific gifts of God are confirmed (II Timothy 1:6). The latter is practiced with great carefulness (I Timothy 5:22). The laying on of hands in confirmation of the gifts of God is of no value unless God has actually conferred the gifts. (See I Timothy 1:18.)

The resurrection of the dead. As Paul wrote, the resurrection of the dead is an essential doctrine of Christianity. "Now if Christ be preached that he rose from the dead, how say some among you that there is no resurrection of the dead? But if there be no resurrection of the dead, then is Christ not risen: And if Christ be not risen, then is our preaching vain, and your faith is also vain" (I Corinthians 15:12-14). (See also I Corinthians 15:4, 15-23.)

Eternal judgment. After the resurrection of the dead, all shall stand before God for judgment (John 5:28-29; Acts 24:15).

The church will be raptured (caught up) to be with Christ at His appearance (I Thessalonians 4:13-18). It appears that following the resurrection and translation of saints when Jesus descends from heaven, a period of seven years relating to the nation of Israel (Daniel 9:24-27; I Corinthians 15:23; I Thessalonians 4:13-18) will fulfill God's plan for Israel. Then the tribulation saints will be raised at the end of that period (Revelation 20:4-5), followed by the Millennium, a period of one thousand years of peace on earth (Revelation 20:1-3; 6-7): All the dead, both small and great, will stand before the Great White Throne for the final judgment (Revelation 20:11-15): All whose names are not found written in the book of life will be cast into the lake of fire.

Summary

The United Pentecostal Church International believes that the Bible is the final authority. It endeavors to teach and live in accordance with the doctrine of the apostles, as shown in the New Testament.

We believe in the *unity of the Scriptures*, that the Word of God does not contradict itself. "The words of the LORD are pure words: as silver tried in a furnace of earth, purified seven times" (Psalm 12:6).

We believe in the *unity of the Spirit*. The Holy Spirit will not contradict the Bible. Instead, the Holy Spirit will "guide you into all truth" (John 16:13).

We believe in the *unity of the faith*. There is but one faith (Ephesians 4:5), and those who walk in the light (I John 1:7) will come to the unity of the faith (Ephesians 4:13).

We believe the church must teach the doctrine of Christ as taught by the apostles and prophets, and this includes the doctrines of repentance, faith toward God, the baptism of water and the baptism of the Holy Ghost, the laying on of hands, the resurrection of the dead, and eternal judgment.

We invite you to join with us as we seek to follow Jesus, who is the "true Light, which lighteth every man that cometh into the world" (John 1:9).

Test Your Knowledge

1. What does the word *doctrine* mean?
2. What three sources of doctrine did we discuss in this chapter?
3. What are the six elements of the doctrine of Christ?
4. What does the word *repent* signify?
5. What two baptisms are included in the "doctrine of baptisms"?
6. What does the name *Jesus* mean?

Apply Your Knowledge

The only practical way a person can apply his knowledge of the true faith is to obey the principles of the doctrine of Christ. Do you have faith in Christ? Have you repented of your sins? Have you been baptized in water in the name of Jesus Christ? Have you received the Holy Ghost, with the initial evidence of speaking with tongues?

Expand Your Knowledge

For further study, consider *Bible Doctrines— Foundation of the Church* from the Word Aflame Publications elective series. A survey of major Bible doctrines, this book will help the student grasp what the Bible itself has to say about salvation, faith, repentance, water baptism, the baptism of the Holy Ghost, and several other important topics.

It would be profitable to read this book as a study help, marking the verses in the Bible to which it refers.

5
The Mighty God in Christ

For in him dwelleth all the fulness of the Godhead bodily.

Colossians 2:9

Start with the Scriptures

Deuteronomy 6:1-9   John 14:1-31
John 1:1-14

The biblical message of the mighty God in Jesus Christ is perhaps the greatest distinctive of the United Pentecostal Church International, distinguishing it from trinitarian Christianity, including trinitarian Pentecostals. This doctrine, commonly known as Oneness, can be defined by two affirmations: (1) There is one God with no distinction of persons; (2) Jesus Christ is all the fullness of the Godhead incarnate. In other words, all titles of the Deity apply to Jesus, and all aspects of the divine personality are manifested in Him.

God's Oneness

The basis of this biblical doctrine is an uncompromising belief in one God, which is known as monotheism. Simply stated, God is absolutely and indivisibly one. There are no essential distinctions or divisions in His eternal nature. All the names and titles of the Deity, such as God, Jehovah (LORD), Lord, Father, Word, and Holy Spirit refer to one and the same being. Any plurality associated with God is only a plurality of attributes, titles, roles, manifestations, modes of activity, or relationships to humanity.

This is the historic position of Judaism. Both Oneness and Jewish believers find the classic expression of this belief in Deuteronomy 6:4: "Hear, O Israel: The LORD our God is one LORD." In subsequent verses, God underscored the importance of this truth by commanding His people to teach it to their children when sitting, walking; lying down, and rising up—in other words, continually. Jesus also emphasized the importance of this teaching, calling it "the first of all the commandments" (Mark 12:29).

Many other biblical passages affirm strict monotheism and exclude any plurality in the Deity. For example:

- "Before me there was no God formed, neither shall there be after me. I, even I, am the LORD; and beside me there is no saviour" (Isaiah 43:10-11).
- "There is no God else beside me; a just God and a Saviour; there is none beside me" (Isaiah 45:21).
- "I am God, and there is none else; I am God, and there is none like me" (Isaiah 46:9).
- "This is life eternal, that they might know thee the only true God, and Jesus Christ, whom thou hast sent" (John 17:3).
- "There is none other God but one. . . . But to us there is but one God, the Father" (I Corinthians 8:4, 6).

57

- "God is one" (Galatians 3:20).
- "For there is one God" (I Timothy 2:5).
- "Thou believest that there is one God; thou doest well: the devils also believe, and tremble" (James 2:19).

Trinitarians sometimes explain that the Old Testament monotheistic passages merely speak of perfect agreement and unity among the trinity, excluding a plurality of false deities but not a plurality of persons in the true God. This view would allow outright polytheism, however, for many distinct deities could exist in perfect harmony.

Neither testament uses the word *trinity* or associates the word *three* or the word *persons* with God in any significant way, but over fifty times the Bible calls God the Holy One. The only New Testament passage to use the word *person* in relation to God is Hebrews 1:3. It says the Son is the image of God's own person (literally "substance"), not a separate person. The only passage to use the word *three* in relation to God is I John 5:7 (KJV), which speaks of three ways in which God has revealed Himself—as Father, Word, and Spirit. It does not imply a plurality of persons any more than when we speak of a man, his word, and his spirit, and it concludes by saying, "These three are one."

The Absolute Deity of Jesus Christ

Jesus Christ is the incarnation of the one God: "For in him dwelleth all the fulness of the Godhead bodily. And ye are complete in him, which is the head of all principality and power" (Colossians 2:9-10). Jesus is not the incarnation of one person of a trinity, but the incarnation of all the character, quality, and personality of the one God.

Jesus is God in the Old Testament sense; that is what New Testament writers meant when they called Jesus God. The one and only God of the Old Testament incarnated Himself as Jesus Christ. "God was in Christ, reconciling the world unto himself" (II Corinthians 5:19). Thomas confessed Jesus as "my Lord and my God" (John 20:28). Jesus is God with us, the eternally blessed God, the image of the invisible God, God manifest in flesh, our God and Savior, and the express image of God's substance. (See Matthew 1:23; Romans 9:5; II Corinthians 4:4; Colossians 1:15; I Timothy 3:16; Titus 2:13; Hebrews 1:3; II Peter 1:1.)

All names and titles of God apply to Jesus.

Jesus is Jehovah. The New Testament applies to Jesus' many Old Testament statements concerning Jehovah. For example, in Isaiah 45:23 Jehovah said, "Unto me every knee shall bow, every tongue shall swear," but in Romans 14:10-11 and Philippians 2:10-11 Paul applied this prophecy to Christ. Jesus said, "Before Abraham was, I am" (John 8:58), referring to the name "I AM" that Jehovah had used for Himself in Exodus 3:14. The Old Testament describes Jehovah as the Almighty, only Savior, Lord of lords, First and Last, only Creator, Holy One, Redeemer, Judge, Shepherd, and Light; yet the New Testament gives all these titles to Jesus Christ.

Jesus is the Father incarnate. "His name shall be called . . . The mighty God, The everlasting Father" (Isaiah 9:6). "Thou, O LORD, art our father, our redeemer" (Isaiah 63:16). "I and my Father are one" (John 10:30). "The Father is in me, and I in him" (John 10:38). "He that hath seen me hath seen the Father" (John 14:9). Jesus is the father of overcomers (Revelation 21:6-7). The Bible attributes many works both to the Father and to Jesus: resurrecting Christ's body, sending the Comforter, drawing men to God, answering prayer, sanctifying believers, and resurrecting the dead.

The Holy Spirit is literally the Spirit that was in Jesus Christ. "The Spirit of truth . . . dwelleth with you, and shall be in you. I will not leave you comfortless: I will come to you" (John 14:17-18). "The Lord is that Spirit" (II Corinthians 3:17). The Holy Spirit is the Spirit of the Son and the Spirit of Jesus Christ (Galatians 4:6; Philippians 1:19). The New Testament ascribes the following works both to Jesus and to the Holy Spirit: moving on prophets of old, resurrection of Christ's body, work as the Comforter (advocate), giving words to believers in time of persecution, intercession, sanctification, and indwelling of believers.

Finally, Jesus is the One on the throne in heaven, as we see by comparing the description of Jesus in Revelation 1 with that of the One on the throne in Revelation 4 and by noting that "God and the Lamb" is one being in Revelation 22:3-4. Trinitarians are often unsure whether they will see one divine being or three divine beings in heaven, but any notion of three visible beings is tritheism (belief in three gods).

Father, Son, and Holy Ghost

The Bible certainly speaks of the Father, Son, and Holy Ghost, but not as three distinct persons. The one God is the Father of all creation, Father of the only begotten Son, and Father of the born-again believer. (See Deuteronomy 32:6; Malachi 2:10.) The title of Son refers to God's incarnation, for the man Christ was literally conceived by the Spirit of God (Matthew 1:18-20; Luke 1:35). The title of Holy Spirit describes the fundamental character of God's nature. Holiness forms the basis of His moral attributes, while spirituality forms the basis of His nonmoral attributes. The title specifically refers to God in activity. (See Genesis 1:2.) It particularly speaks of God as He anoints, regenerates, and dwells in humans.

Thus, the titles of Father, Son, and Spirit describe God's multiple roles and works, but they do not reflect an essential threeness in God's nature, and all apply simultaneously to Jesus. The terms can also be understood in God's revelation to humanity: *Father* refers to God in family relationship to humanity; *Son* refers to God in flesh; and *Spirit* refers to God in activity. For example, one man can have three significant relationships or functions—such as administrator, teacher, and counsellor—and yet be one person in every sense of the word. God is not defined by or limited to an essential threeness.

The Bible identifies the Father and the Holy Spirit as one and the same being. The title of Holy Spirit simply describes what the Father is. God is an invisible Spirit (John 4:24). The Holy Spirit is literally the Father of Jesus, since Jesus was conceived by the Holy Spirit (Matthew 1:18, 20). The Bible calls the Holy Spirit the Spirit of Jehovah, the Spirit of God, and the Spirit of the Father (Matthew 10:20). The Bible attributes many works of the Father to the Spirit as well, such as resurrecting Christ and indwelling, comforting, sanctifying, and resurrecting believers.

In order to understand the concept of Oneness more fully, let us examine some scriptural passages often cited in support of trinitarianism.

The baptism of Christ did not introduce to the devout Jewish onlookers a radical, innovative doctrine of plurality in the Godhead, but it signified the authoritative anointing of Jesus as the Messiah. The dove was a sign for John, and the voice was a sign for the people. A correct understanding of God's omnipresence and omnipotence dispels any notion that the heavenly voice and dove require separate persons.

Christ's description of the Holy Ghost as "another Comforter" in John 14 indicates a difference of form or relationship, that is, Christ in Spirit rather than in flesh.

The New Testament speaks of Jesus as being at the right hand of God. This phrase does not denote a physical positioning of two beings with two bodies, for God is a Spirit and does not have a physical body outside of Jesus Christ. This view would be indistinguishable from belief in two gods. Rather, the phrase is an idiomatic expression from the Old Testament denoting that Christ possesses all the power, authority, and preeminence of God and describing His present mediatorial role because of the Cross.

Similarly, the vision of the One on the throne and the Lamb in Revelation 5 is symbolic only. The One on the throne represents all the Deity, while the Lamb represents the Son in His human, sacrificial role.

The Son

As we have seen, the Son is the manifestation of the one God in flesh. The title of Son can refer to the human nature of Christ alone (as in "the Son died") or to the union of deity and humanity (as in "the Son shall return to earth in glory.") It is never used apart from God's incarnation, however; it never refers to deity alone. The phrases "God the Son" and "eternal Son" are nonbiblical. The Son was begotten by the miraculous work of the Holy Spirit in the womb of the virgin Mary. The following verses show that the Son had a beginning:

- "The Holy Ghost shall come upon thee, and the power of the Highest shall overshadow thee: therefore also that holy thing which shall be born of thee shall be called the Son of God" (Luke 1:35).

- "But when the fulness of the time was come, God sent forth his Son, made of a woman, made under the law" (Galatians 4:4).
- "Thou art my Son, this day have I begotten thee. . . . I will be to him a Father, and he shall be to me a Son" (Hebrews 1:5).

One day the distinctive role of the Son will end, when the redemptive purpose for which God manifested Himself in flesh is fulfilled. God will continue to reveal Himself through the immortal, glorified human body of Christ, but the mediatorial work and reign of the Son will end. The role of the Son will be submerged back into the greatness of God, who will remain in His original role as Father, Creator, and Lord of all. "Then shall the Son also himself be subject unto him that put all things under him, that God may be all in all" (I Corinthians 15:28).

Not only must we acknowledge the one true God of the Old Testament—the Father and Creator—but we must also acknowledge His revelation in flesh, as Jesus Christ. Salvation does not come to us simply because God is Spirit, but specifically through the atoning death of the man Christ Jesus. That is why John 17:3 says that to be saved we must not only know the one true God but also Jesus Christ, whom He sent. This concept also explains the typical greeting in Paul's epistles: "Grace to you and peace from God our Father, and the Lord Jesus Christ" (Romans 1:7). Likewise, I Timothy 2:5 says there is "one God, and one mediator between God and men, the man Christ Jesus." A second divine person is not our mediator; the Man who became a sacrifice for our sins is our mediator with God.

Jesus is both God and man at the same time. This truth explains the plural references to Father and Son in the Gospels. As Father, Jesus sometimes acted and spoke from His divine self-consciousness;

as Son He sometimes acted and spoke from His human self-consciousness. For example, as a man He was tempted, hungry, thirsty, grew weary, suffered, and died. But as God He forgave sin, performed creative miracles, and took authority over disease, demons, and death.

The prayers of Christ demonstrate the struggle of the human will as it submitted to the divine will. Jesus prayed from His human self-consciousness, not as a second divine person, for by definition God does not need to pray. Speaking of His humanity, Jesus frequently stated that the Son was inferior to the Father in power, authority, and knowledge. If these examples demonstrated a plurality of persons, they would establish the subordination of one person to the other, contrary to the trinitarian doctrine of co-equality.

According to Hebrews 1:2, God made the worlds by the Son. Certainly, the Spirit of God who dwelt in the Son was the Creator. Moreover, God based the entire work of creation upon the future manifestation of the Son. God foreknew that humans would sin, but He also foreknew that through the Son they could be saved and could fulfill His original purpose in creation. Though God did not pick up the humanity until the fullness of time, He acted upon it from all eternity. The Lamb was "foreordained before the foundation of the world, but was manifest in these last times" (I Peter 1:20). Jesus did not pre-exist the Incarnation as an eternal Son but as the eternal Spirit of God.

The Word in John 1 is not equivalent to the title of Son, for the latter is limited to the Incarnation while the former is not. The Word is God's self-revelation, self-expression, or self disclosure. Before the Incarnation, the Word was the unexpressed thought, plan, or mind of God. In the beginning, the Word was with God, not as a separate person but as God

Himself—pertaining to and belonging to God much like a man and his word. In the fullness of time God put flesh on the Word; He revealed Himself in flesh.

The Name of Jesus

Both testaments place strong emphasis on the doctrine of the name of God. For people in biblical times, a name was an extension of an individual's personality. Specifically, the name of God represents the revelation of His presence, character, power, and authority. In the Old Testament, Jehovah was the redemptive name of God and the unique name by which He distinguished Himself from false gods. In the New Testament, however, God accompanied the revelation of Himself in flesh with a new name. That name is Jesus, which includes and supersedes Jehovah, since it literally means Jehovah-Savior or Jehovah is Salvation. Although others have borne the name Jesus, the Lord Jesus Christ is the only one who is actually what that name describes.

Jesus is the redemptive name of God in the New Testament. It carries the power and authority needed by the church, as shown by the following passages of Scripture:

- "If ye shall ask any thing in my name, I will do it" (John 14:14).

- "Neither is there salvation in any other: for there is none other name under heaven given among men, whereby we must be saved" (Acts 4:12).

- "Through his name whosoever believeth in him shall receive remission of sins" (Acts 10:43).

- "Wherefore God also hath highly exalted him, and given him a name which is above every name: That at the name of Jesus every knee should bow, of things in heaven, and things in earth, and things under the earth" (Philippians 2:9-10).

- "Whatsoever ye do in word or deed, do all in the name of the Lord Jesus" (Colossians 3:17).

The early church prayed, preached, taught, healed the sick, performed miracles, cast out unclean spirits, and baptized in the name of Jesus. The name of Jesus is not a magical formula; it is effective only through faith in Jesus and a relationship with Him. Nevertheless, the Christian should actually use the spoken name Jesus in prayer and baptism as an outward expression of faith in Jesus and in obedience to God's Word.

Conclusion

In contrast to trinitarianism, Oneness asserts that (1) God is indivisibly one in number with no distinction of persons; (2) Jesus is the absolute fullness of the Godhead in flesh; He is God, Jehovah, Father; Son; and Holy Spirit; (3) the Son of God was begotten after the flesh and did not exist from eternity past—the term only refers to God's incarnation in Christ; (4) the Word is not a separate person, but the mind, thought, plan, or expression of the Father; (5) Jesus is the revealed name of God in the New Testament and represents salvation, power, and authority from God; (6) water baptism should be administered by orally invoking the name Jesus as part of the baptismal formula; and (7) believers will see only one divine being in heaven: Jesus Christ.

Test Your Knowledge

1. What Old Testament passage proclaims, "Hear, O Israel: The LORD our God is one LORD''?

2. Is Jesus in the Godhead, or is the Godhead in Jesus? Explain.

3. Explain what the titles of Father, Son, and Holy Ghost mean.

4. Explain the distinction between the Father and the Son and give scriptural examples.

5. Define the Oneness doctrine.

6. Cite three scriptural references that declare Jesus to be the one God incarnate.

Apply Your Knowledge

The Oneness doctrine is important because it upholds biblical Christianity in at least three specific ways: (1) It restores biblical terms and patterns of thought on the subject of the Godhead, clearly establishing New Testament Christianity as the spiritual heir of Old Testament Judaism. (2) It upholds the absolute deity of Jesus Christ, revealing His true identity. (3) It places biblical emphasis on the name of Jesus, making the power of His name available to the believer.

Not only must we know and believe this truth, but in view of its crucial significance, we must propagate it everywhere. The church has the responsibility to teach this message from the pulpit, in the Sunday school, and through Bible studies. Each believer also has the responsibility to share it with others. And parents have a particular responsibility to teach it to their children.

In short, the message of the mighty God in Jesus Christ is vital to restoring biblical belief and apostolic power.

Expand Your Knowledge

For further study, see the following Word Aflame Press books:

- *The Oneness of God* by David K. Bernard
- *The God of Two Testaments* by Robert Brent Graves
- *Is Jesus in the Godhead, or Is the Godhead in Jesus?* by Gordon Magee

6
Pentecostal Worship

O magnify the LORD with me, and let us exalt his name together.

Psalm 34:3

Start with the Scriptures

Psalm 150
Amos 9:11-12

Acts 15:13-19
I Thessalonians 5:18

Pentecostal worship, when contrasted with the worship of many contemporary churches, is rather different. The verbal congregational expressions in praise and prayer, the significant role of singing and musical instruments, the physical demonstrations in worship, and the energetic preaching may appear to the stoic as irreverent. Formal denominations consider the church service to be a place for deep meditation, silent introspection, restrained participation, and pious formalities. Pentecostals, although they respect these methods and agree that they have their place, believe that the church service is a celebration—the believers are the celebrants and Jesus is the celebrity! Therefore, the atmosphere is alive with joyous expressions that celebrate the majestic splendor of God.

What Is Pentecostal Worship?

A believer, upon conversion, becomes a minister for the Lord. We are not referring to a preaching type ministry, but we are saying that each individual has a place of function and influence in the church. Paul compared the members of the church to a physical body, with each individual functioning in some vital way, ministering to that body (I Corinthians 12:12-27).

Our ministering can be divided into three basic areas—*exhortation*, *evangelism*, and *worship*. Let's look at each of these briefly.

Exhortation is the ministry we render to our spiritual brothers and sisters. We pray for, comfort, assist, encourage, counsel, and protect one another (I Thessalonians 5:6-11).

Evangelism is the ministry we offer to the sinner. This ministry reaches for the lost through intercessory prayer, witnessing, providing good examples, being a friend, and sharing the Word of God (Matthew 28:19; Mark 16:15).

The third ministry is different from the other two because it does not directly involve others. *Worship* is a direct ministry to the Lord. It is not horizontal (i.e., reaching to people), but vertical—reaching directly to God. Worship is an interaction between the believer and God, without the involvement of anyone else. Of course, we can encourage one another in worship, but ultimately the experience is between the believer and God. It is a wonderful thought to consider that God is actually gratified when we worship Him. We are actually ministering unto the Lord when we worship Him.

Worship can be broken down into three progressive steps: *thanksgiving*, *praise*, and *worship*.

To be a worshiper we have to start with an attitude of gratitude. Thanksgiving is that prevailing thankful attitude that creates the seeding ground for a great worshipful experience with God. If we are an unthankful person, we will never become a good worshiper. In fact, Romans 1 describes the serious problems that result from an unthankful heart. Thanksgiving is a prevailing mental state of gratitude for what God *has done*. Paul said, "In every thing give thanks: for this is the will of God in Christ Jesus concerning you" (I Thessalonians 5:18).

Praise goes one step further and expresses that gratitude in some verbal, audible or demonstrative way. Praise can be heard. Verbally or demonstratively extolling the virtues and divine attributes of God is praise. Thanksgiving praises Him for *what He has done* and praise exalts Him for *who He is*. All expressions of praise can be grouped in these three areas.

Verbal. "My tongue shall speak of thy righteousness and of thy praise all the day long" (Psalm 35:28). (See also Psalm 40:3; 89:1; 119:108; 119:171; Isaiah 12:6; Hebrews 13:15; Revelation 19:1.)

Audible. "Praise the LORD with harp: sing unto him with the psaltery, and an instrument of ten strings" (Psalm 33:2). "O clap your hands, all ye people; shout unto God with the voice of triumph" (Psalm 47:1). "Praise him with the sound of the trumpet . . . psaltery and harp . . . timbrel and dance . . . stringed instruments and organs . . . cymbals . . ." (Psalm 150:3-5). (See also Exodus 15:20; II Chronicles 5:13.)

Demonstrative. "I will lift up my hands in thy name" (Psalm 63:4). "And he leaping up stood and walked, and entered with them into the temple, walking, and leaping, and praising God" (Acts 3:8). "Let them praise his name in the dance" (Psalm 149:3).

Worship is the ultimate in this interaction with God—the apex of divine communion. This third and highest level of ministry unto the Lord that we are calling "worship" is not just man reaching to God, but it is a mutual exchange between God and man. Worship enters the supernatural realm where there is real contact with the Spirit of God. Worship is entering the throne room of God and bowing in His presence.

The Roots of Pentecostal Worship

Pentecostal worship finds its roots in the apostolic pattern. The early church forms the design and basis for our entire belief system. The church today is an extension of that pristine church of the first century, born on the Day of Pentecost (Ephesians 2:20). We are worshiping the same Jesus and have been baptized in the same Spirit as the early church.

Information is sparse as to how the early church worshiped. There are only hints, at best, as to the methods they employed in a normal church service. In contrast to this, the Old Testament is replete with information concerning praise and worship methods. This absence of instruction in the New Testament indicates that the resurrection of Jesus and the indwelling Holy Ghost make following mechanical instructions unnecessary for one to worship God. Our praise and worship is spontaneous, heartfelt expression—not adherence to demanded ceremony and ritual.

The following points can be made concerning worship in the first century:

Since the early church was Jewish, Old Testament worship methods were most likely adopted in apostolic worship. "Christianity began among the Aramaic-speaking Jews and then spread to the Hellenistic Jewish community and eventually to the Gentiles," according to Robert Webber in *Worship Old and New.*

The worship methods of David's tabernacle continued to be the expression of the apostolic church. David's tabernacle was a very unusual interjection into the Old Testament system. While Moses' tabernacle was located at Shiloh, where the priests continued their sacrifices, David's tabernacle was located in Jerusalem on Mount Zion. David's tabernacle was a tent in which dwelt the ark of the covenant. It was surrounded with choirs and orchestras offering praise twenty-four hours a day, seven days a week (I Chronicles 15; 16; 25). God permitted this unprecedented phenomenon and made it a prophetic display of His coming kingdom.

Amos prophesied the tabernacle of David would be restored (Amos 9:11-12) and James confirmed that its fulfillment was being experienced in the first-century church, which began on the Day of Pentecost (Acts 15:13-16). Part of this restoration was the adoption of David's worship methods—singing, musical instruments, dancing, clapping, lifting hands, and others. Pentecostal worship, therefore, is based upon the apostolic pattern, which inherited its practice from its rich Jewish heritage.

The Methods of Pentecostal Worship

We can become so preoccupied with the methods of worship that we forget the real purpose. Nevertheless, Pentecostal worship methods are sometimes challenged, so we defend them from a biblical point of view. We want to examine them, not to be technical, but to establish the boundaries of proper expression.

72

We will examine the physical expressions of biblical worship as well as events that create a climate for worship.

Physical Expressions of Worship

Physical expressions of worship involve offering our bodies as an offering of praise unto the Lord. Paul said our bodies are the temple of God. "Therefore glorify God in your body, and in your spirit, which are God's" (I Corinthians 6:20).

• *Our mouth* is possibly the most frequently used physical organ of praise.

> Talking: "My tongue also shall talk of thy righteousness all the day long" (Psalm 71:24). (See also Psalm 77:12; 119:27.)

> Shouting: "Shout unto God with the voice of triumph" (Psalm 47:1). (See also II Chronicles 20:19; Luke 19:37; Revelation 5:11-12.)

> Singing: "Sing praises to God, sing praises: sing praises unto our King, sing praises" (Psalm 47:6). (See also Psalm 66:4; Matthew 26:30; Acts 16:25; Hebrews 2:12.)

> Laughter: "Then was our mouth filled with laughter, and our tongue with singing" (Psalm 126:2). Seven times the psalmist said, "Make a joyful noise unto God" (Psalm 66:1; 81:1; 95:1-2; 98:4, 6; 100:1). This would include laughter.

> Tongues: "For he that speaketh in an unknown tongue speaketh not unto men, but unto God" (I Corinthians 14:2). (See also I Corinthians 14:14-15; Jude 20.)

• *Our hands* are very useful in worship and praise to the Lord:

> Lifting hands: "I lift up my hands toward thy holy oracle" (Psalm 28:2). (See also Psalm 63:4; 134:2; I Timothy 2:8.)

Clapping hands: "O clap your hands, all ye people" (Psalm 47:1). (See also Psalm 98:8; Isaiah 55:12:)

- *Our feet* are also useful in praise and worship:
Stand: "My foot standeth in an even place: in the congregations will I bless the LORD" (Psalm 26:12). (See also Psalm 134:1; 135:1-2.)
Walking, running and leaping: "And he leaping up stood, and walked, and entered with them into the temple, walking, and leaping, and praising God" (Acts 3:8). (See also Luke 6:23; II Samuel 22:29-30; Psalm 18:29.)
Dancing: "Let them praise his name in the dance" (Psalm 149:3). (See also Psalm 150:4; I Chronicles 15:29; Exodus 15:20:)

- *Our entire body* is an instrument of praise and worship.
Bowing and kneeling: "For this cause I bow my knees unto the Father of our Lord Jesus Christ" (Ephesians 3:14). (See also Psalm 95:6; Genesis 24:48; I Chronicles 29:20; Daniel 6:10; Matthew 17:14-15.)
Prostration: "And when I saw him, I fell at his feet as dead. And he laid his right hand upon me" (Revelation 1:17). (See also Mark 5:22; Luke 5:12; Acts 9:3-4.)

Three common methods by which we may worship are singing, playing musical instruments unto the Lord, and in giving of our finances.

Singing of hymns. In Acts 4:24; "They lifted up their voice to God with one accord, and said. . . ." Six verses of beautiful praise follow, possibly recording the words of a hymn, otherwise they could not have lifted their voices with one accord. A song puts amplitude to our words of praise. (See Ephesians 5:19; I Corinthians 14:15; Acts 16:25; Colossians 3:16; James 5:13.)

Playing of musical instruments. Even though there is no explicit command in the New Testament to use musical instruments in worship, we know it is an appropriate method. With such profuse use of musical instruments in the Old Testament, it seems obvious that if the Lord did not like musical instruments in worship He would have said so. The Greek word *psallo* is used four times in the New Testament, directly associated with praise, and it means "to twitch, twang, to play a stringed instrument with the fingers." The word is translated "making melody" (Ephesians 5:19) and "sing" (Romans 15:9; I Corinthians 14:15; James 5:13). If God had intended that the praise not be accompanied by musical instruments He would have inspired the use of the Greek word *ado*, which means only to sing. The early church was obviously accustomed to the use of musical instruments (I Corinthians 13:1; 14:7-8).

Offerings. Giving money in the offering should be as praise and worship unto the Lord. "Every man according as he purposeth in his heart, so let him give; not grudgingly, or of necessity: for God loveth a cheerful giver" (II Corinthians 9:7).

Events That Create a Climate Conducive to Worship

Preaching and teaching. Both of these events recreate the gospel story, giving the listener an opportunity to involve himself in worship. The first Easter message is recorded in Acts 2. Peter exalted the Lord through preaching, and 3,000 people were converted. Also, in the fourth chapter of Acts, 5,000 people were converted by the preaching of John and Peter. Preaching and teaching that exalt Jesus Christ create a climate of worship.

Communion. Just as the Passover was the fulcrum of Old Testament rituals, the communion service replaced it as a Christian ordinance. "For even Christ our passover is sacrificed for us" (I Corinthians 5:7). Jesus instituted this memorial in Matthew 26:22-30. Its importance was emphasized by Paul the apostle in I Corinthians 11:23-34. Communion reminds us of the sacrificial death of Jesus and symbolizes a oneness between the believer and Jesus, thereby stimulating heartfelt worship.

Foot washing. Washing one another's feet was instituted by the Lord Jesus (John 13:1-20). After Jesus had washed the disciples feet He said, "If I then, your Lord and Master, have washed your feet; ye also ought to wash one another's feet" (John 13:14). The historical customs of that day made foot washing more relevant, yet when practiced today foot washing revives a basic principle of God's kingdom—the greatness of servanthood. A worshiper must assume the role of servanthood before he can be a true worshiper. Foot washing does not guarantee servanthood, but it is symbolical and reminds us that we are servants of each other to the glory of God.

Baptism. Even though baptism is a one-time experience and is a part of conversion, it is a beautiful act that elicits praise and worship from the believer (Acts 2:38; 8:12;10:47; 19:5). It dramatizes the burial of the old man that died in repentance—doing symbolically what Jesus did literally (Colossians 2:12; Romans 6:4). It also symbolizes and in truth initiates the washing away of all our sins by the blood of Jesus Christ (Acts 2:38; 22:16).

Special days. Paul said, "Let no man therefore judge you in meat, or in drink, or in respect of an holyday, or of the new moon, or of the sabbath days: which are a shadow of things to come" (Colossians 2:16-17). Although there are no

Christian holidays established in the Bible, there are convenient times to celebrate certain Christian beliefs. One traditional Christian special day is Sunday. The Jewish Sabbath is Saturday, which is the seventh day of the week. But Christians worship on Sunday in order to celebrate the resurrection of Jesus, which occurred on the first day of the week. Sunday is not a holy day, but a convenient day in our society to conduct worship services and to serve as a day of rest.

Salutation. Worshipful greetings are biblical. When Boaz arrived from Bethlehem he greeted the harvesters with, "The LORD be with you," and they called back, "The LORD bless thee" (Ruth 2:4). When greeting another believer, it is a good opportunity to offer a hearty, "Praise the Lord!"

Testimonies. Public testimonies of praise in the church service have been practiced by Pentecostals for years. Many have referred to the verse of Scripture in Revelation 12:11: "And they overcame him by the blood of the Lamb, and by the word of their testimony." Although this passage is concerning martyrs during the tribulation, the principle is illustrated here that there is power in testifying for the Lord.

Altar service. This is a time for the saints to make consecrations and commitments to the challenges given by the Holy Ghost in the service. It is also a time for sinners to find salvation. This makes the altar service a wonderful time of worship and praise. Worship creates the climate for sinners to be converted at our altars.

The Pentecostal Experience and Worship

It is not just happenstance that the Pentecostal churches are the ones that practice biblical methods of worship with exuberance and enthusiasm. The churches that forbid many biblical worship methods are the same churches that denounce the Pentecostal experience as being available today.

David's tabernacle. The outpouring of the Holy Ghost in Acts 2 was the fulfillment of many Old Testament prophecies. Yet one outstanding prophecy, given by Amos, links the Pentecostal experience and worship together in an interesting relationship of fulfillment. Amos prophesied that the tabernacle of David would be restored, and James confirmed that the events of the apostolic era was a fulfillment of that restoration (Amos 9:11-12; Acts 15:13-19).

The following points can be made concerning the prophetic fulfillment of David's tabernacle, as it relates to worship in the Pentecostal experience:

- David's tabernacle was an open tent.
- The worship practiced at David's tabernacle was spontaneous and unrestrained.
- David, in his tabernacle, organized music and made it a permanent part of the worship experience.
- The ark of the covenant and not sacrificial rituals became a focus of worship.

The Feast of Pentecost. The New Testament Pentecost fell on the same day as the Old Testament Pentecost (Acts 2:1). The Feast of Pentecost was the fiftieth day after the Feast of the Passover. It was a dual celebration, the celebration of the harvest season and a commemoration of the giving of the law at Mount Sinai. The outpouring of the Holy Ghost fulfilled both celebrations. What a harvest on that first day—3,120 souls were made members of the church (Acts 1:15; 2:41). Pentecost is also a celebration of a better way! The second Pentecost is saturated with praise and worship to God because it is the event that marked the beginning of the new covenant.

Pentecostal Music and Worship

Most Pentecostal churches use music extensively in worship. We are living in a musically-saturated society. Modern technology has made more music available than at any other time in history. Therefore, since music was used in biblical praise, it is appropriate that it be used abundantly in worship today.

A survey of biblical music will reveal that sacred music was used for praise and worship. Music can be used for teaching, witnessing, and entertainment, but biblically it is for worship.

Test Your Knowledge

True or False

_____ 1. Dancing is not a form of New Testament worship since it was an Old Testament practice only.

_____ 2. Thanksgiving is a primary attitude of gratitude forming the essential basis for real praise and worship.

_____ 3. Praise is a deep, silent meditation upon God.

_____ 4. True spiritual worship transcends the physical and becomes a spiritual interaction between God and man.

_____ 5. Pentecostal methods of worship are the result of traditions established by highly emotional founders at the turn of the century.

_____ 6. If Christians work for God and serve Him horizontally through evangelism and edification, worship becomes unnecessary.

_____ 7. Praise can be expressed either verbally, audibly, or demonstratively

_____ 8. Since the early church was Jewish and Jesus was the Jewish Messiah fulfilling all the Old Testament types, many methods of worship in the Old Testament were adopted in the worship of the Lord Jesus Christ.

_____ 9. The restoration of David's tabernacle was fulfilled when Gentiles were allowed into the church and has no further significance.

_____ 10. The outpouring of the Holy Ghost on the Day of Pentecost stands in great contrast to the Feast of Pentecost as an event of celebration.

Apply Your Knowledge

If leaving a service feeling down and defeated. describes your consistent experience, it would be good to evaluate your worship involvement.

If you are an inhibited person, offering a sacrifice of praise using biblical methods will open up new avenues of expression to you. You will be liberated from your prison of self-consciousness and will experience great heights of joyous praise and worship.

It is also good to expand your vocabulary of worship expressions by reading and memorizing the psalms. Learning to recall the virtues and attributes of God will expand and inspire your praise. Learning new choruses is a wonderful way to add freshness to your worship.

Expand Your Knowledge

There are many books on praise and worship. Here are two that we recommend:

- *A Look at Pentecostal Worship* from the Word Aflame Publications elective series.
- *Pentecostal Worship* by Gary D. Erickson (Word Aflame Press).

Both of these books may be ordered from the Pentecostal Publishing House.

Pentecostal Lifestyle 7

> *Having therefore these promises, dearly beloved, let us cleanse ourselves from all filthiness of the, flesh and spirit, perfecting holiness in the fear of God.*
>
> *II Corinthians 7:1*

Start with the Scriptures

Genesis 1:27
Matthew 6:19-21
Luke 12:29-31

Romans 12:1-2
Titus 2:11-12
Hebrews 12:14
I Peter 2:21-23

On the sixth day of Creation, when God created man, He did so with extreme care. He made man in His own image. "So God created man in his own image, in the image of God created he him; male and female created he them" (Genesis 1:27). Man was made to worship God, to fellowship with Him, and to bring glory to Him. Man was made for high purposes and with lofty ambitions.

Mankind, through Satan's temptations and Adam and Eve's subsequent yielding, entered into a lifestyle of living below his original privilege and purpose. Only as mankind returns to the first pattern of Creation—made in God's image—will true peace and happiness be his.

Jesus Christ—Our Pattern

As Jesus Christ walked on this earth and lived His exemplary lifestyle, He set a pattern for man to follow. By living in a Christ-like manner as His indwelling Spirit enables us, we find real contentment, joyful living, and fulfillment of purpose.

The world is different from what it was in the first century. However, the same "spirit of holiness" that was in the early church is in the United Pentecostal Church International. In an age of pleasure, compromise, and promiscuity, the United Pentecostal Church members are endeavoring to keep themselves unspotted from the world. Though they are "in the world," they are not "of the world."

Every Christian needs to seek things that are of God rather than things that are of this earth. What speaks more clearly to us, things set apart unto God, or things set apart unto this world? What system of values do we live by: God's values or the carnal values of this world? Jesus said, "Lay not up for yourselves treasures upon earth, where moth and rust doth corrupt, and where thieves break through and steal: But lay up for yourselves treasures in heaven, where neither moth nor rust doth corrupt, and where thieves do not break through nor steal: For where your treasure is, there will your heart be also" (Matthew 6:19-21).

The world urges us to become preoccupied with *getting*, while God's system urges us to be preoccupied with *giving*. Paul told the leaders at Ephesus, "I have shewed you all things, how that so labouring ye ought to support the weak, and to remember the words of the Lord Jesus, how he said, It is more blessed to give than to receive" (Acts 20:35).

Jesus said, "And seek not ye what ye shall eat, or what ye shall drink, neither be ye of doubtful mind. For all these things do the nations of the world seek after: and your Father knoweth that ye have need of these things. But rather seek ye the kingdom of God; and all these things shall be added unto you" (Luke 12:29-31).

The lifestyle that Jesus Christ designed for His church is vastly different from a lifestyle of sin. But Jesus does not demand of us a lifestyle that we cannot live. He has provided the inner transformation and the power for us to live the lifestyle that pleases Him. One's life can be transformed into a new creation in Christ Jesus. Old sinful habits and carnal strivings pass away and a new life of holiness begins. (See II Corinthians 5:17.)

This transformation is more than a possibility. It is a commandment. By seeking the things of God, by faith and obedience to Him, we move toward this transformation that God then performs in us.

"I beseech you therefore, brethren, by the mercies of God, that ye present your bodies a living sacrifice, holy, acceptable unto God, which is your reasonable service. And be not conformed to this world: but be ye transformed by the renewing of your mind, that ye may prove what is that good, and acceptable, and perfect, will of God" (Romans 12:1-2).

Holiness

There are two things that we must do in order to see the Lord. We must follow peace with all men, and we must follow holiness. "Follow peace with all men, and holiness, without which no man shall see the Lord" (Hebrews 12:14).

In order to "follow holiness," we need to understand the meaning of the term holiness. In its efforts to apply the biblical principles of holiness to our lives, the United Pentecostal Church has offered insight into the meaning of holiness to us. The following passage is taken from one section entitled "Holiness" in the Articles of Faith of the United Pentecostal Church International.

Godly living should characterize the life of every child of the Lord, and we should live according to the pattern and example given in the Word of God. "For the grace of God that bringeth salvation hath appeared to all men, Teaching us that, denying ungodliness and worldly lusts, we should live soberly, righteously, and godly, in this present world" (Titus 2:11-12).

"For even hereunto were ye called: because Christ also suffered for us, leaving us an example, that ye should follow his steps: Who did no sin, neither was guile found in his mouth: Who, when he was reviled, reviled not again; when he suffered, he threatened not; but committed himself to him that judgeth righteously" (I Peter 2:21-23).

"Follow peace with all men, and holiness, without which no man shall see the Lord" (Hebrews 12:14).

"But as he which hath called you is holy, so be ye holy in all manner of conversation; because it is written, Be ye holy; for I am holy. And if ye call on the Father, who without respect of persons judgeth according to every man's work, pass the time of your sojourning here in fear: Forasmuch as ye know that ye were not redeemed with corruptible things, as silver and gold, from your vain conversation received by tradi-

tion from your fathers; But with the pre-
cious blood of Christ, as of a lamb without
blemish and without spot" (I Peter 1:15-19).

We wholeheartedly disapprove of our
people indulging in any activities which are
not conducive to good Christianity and
godly living, such as theatres, dances, mixed
bathing, women cutting their hair, make-up,
any worldly sports and amusements, and
unwholesome radio programs and music.
Furthermore, because of the display of all of
these evils on television, we disapprove of
any of our people having television sets in
their homes. We admonish all of our people
to refrain from any of these practices in the
interest of spiritual progress and the soon
coming of the Lord for His church.

While this passage is not intended to be a complete expression of a holy lifestyle, it does mention
several areas in which the UPCI has taken a unified
stand regarding holiness. The specific application
of holiness principles are often referred to as standards of behavior or conduct.

These "standards" of holiness are invaluable to a
person endeavoring to live a lifestyle that is pleasing
to God. In order to better represent Jesus Christ to
the world, the believer seeks to be identified with
Him. Rather than drawing attention to self, flesh, or
worldly attractions, the follower of Christ will boldly
lift up the standard of holiness that serves to identify
him with Christ. Just as a soldier's flag or standard
identifies him and his loyalties to his country, so does
the Christian's identify him with his Savior. A holy
lifestyle is one of the church's most distinctive assets.

Source of Standards

Where do these standards come from? The following excerpts from a Word Aflame Publications book entitled, *Why? A Study of Christian Standards*, lists five sources for holiness standards.

"*The Word of God sets standards*. The Word of God is the mind of God. It expresses to us the will of God for humanity, as well as revealing the history of God's dealing with men. When we know how God thinks concerning the issues of life, we should have little doubt as to His standards. This knowledge of God's will through His Word is a great treasure to the Christian (Jeremiah 9:23-24; Proverbs 2:1-12).

"*The Spirit of God sets standards*. There are times when we do not understand what the Bible teaches about certain modern philosophies. The Spirit will often quicken our minds to certain verses of Scripture or reveal certain things as harmful to our spiritual well-being. These times of prompting by the Spirit are referred to as conviction.

"Many years ago, when the Pentecostal movement first began in North America, people did not know that tobacco causes cancer. Many, however, felt convicted by the Spirit that it was wrong to use tobacco in any form. The use of tobacco was not dealt with directly by the Bible, but verses of Scripture such as 'Let us cleanse ourselves from all filthiness of the flesh and spirit' (II Corinthians 7:1) were quickened to their minds. They considered this habit as filthy to the flesh. Only recently was it proven that tobacco is harmful to the body, but God had convicted His people about it many years ago.

"God dealt with His people in a similar fashion concerning television. It looked like a promising tool of communication when it first emerged, and much of the programming at that time could not be proven to be harmful. But God knew how it would rapidly deteriorate into one of the most influential tools the devil has yet used.

"Many people felt a conviction by the Spirit against television when it was first introduced. Now it is obvious, even to the world, that it has been a bad influence upon our society. For years many people were ridiculed by the world for being against television. Now, more and more of those who embraced television are beginning to fight against it as they, too, see its harmful influence.

"*Tradition sets standards.* Many people who have departed from formal denominations fear tradition. However, there are many traditions that are good to keep. Paul often admonished Christians to 'hold the traditions which ye have been taught' (II Thessalonians 2:15). He also taught them to 'withdraw yourselves from every brother that walketh disorderly, and not after the tradition which he received of us' (II Thessalonians 3:6). He praised the Corinthians for keeping the traditions (ordinances) as he had delivered them (I Corinthians 11:2).

"Sometimes certain standards may be set in the church that are not specifically dealt with in the Scriptures. We must not be quick to discredit traditional standards. Remember that much time, consideration, and prayer have usually gone into the decision to take such a stand.

"The standard is generally built upon the foundation of some principle of God and should not be considered lightly. There is safety in the multitude of counsel (Proverbs 11:14). It is wise to revere and respect standards that have made their way into our traditions.

"*Culture sets standards.* Under some cultures the lighting of a candle in church speaks of praying for the dead. In those areas it would be inappropriate to have a candlelight consecration service. Those who had come from this cultural background would be confused and perhaps tempted to pray for their dead.

"Paul dealt with these same problems in regard to eating meat offered to idols. (See I Corinthians 8; Romans 14.) The culture itself dictated certain standards that the church had to set in order to remain free of reproach.

"We have faced the same problems in our day with dress and hairstyles. Sometimes the church has found it needful to set standards simply to avoid association with certain elements that were not Christian. There are times that this is necessary in order to maintain the separation from the world that God has ordained for His church.

"*The individual sets standards.* Every Christian should have certain convictions that fit his own life. Some people have found themselves craving certain things, such as coffee or soft drinks. They felt that they should not allow such things to control their lives and thus laid them aside in self-discipline. That is commendable; however, that person should not make such standards universal.

"Standards are not an end in themselves. When that becomes the case, we become guilty of the world's charge of legalism. We are not to be legalistic. Standards do not save us. They are merely tools to draw attention to the right things, to help us live a life that will save us, and to give direction and order to our lives."

Attitudes—Beatitudes

In seeking to understand the lifestyle of a Pentecostal person, a brief consideration of the Beatitudes is in order. Jesus, in His teaching of the Sermon on the Mount, offered several patterns for living an overcoming Christian life.

"Blessed are the poor in spirit: for theirs is the kingdom of heaven.

"Blessed are they that mourn: for they shall be comforted.

"Blessed are the meek: for they shall inherit the earth.

"Blessed are they which do hunger and thirst after righteousness: for they shall be filled.

"Blessed are the merciful: for they shall obtain mercy.

"Blessed are the pure in heart: for they shall see God.

"Blessed are the peacemakers: for they shall be called the children of God.

"Blessed are they which are persecuted for righteousness' sake: for theirs is the kingdom of heaven.

"Blessed are ye, when men shall revile you, and persecute you, and shall say all manner of evil against you falsely, for my sake" (Matthew 5:3-11).

These Beatitudes, as well as the remainder of the Sermon on the Mount, are Christ's teachings regarding the lifestyle that He is pleased with. As a person fulfills these instructions through the power of Christ in him, he will be living a "Pentecostal lifestyle."

Test Your Knowledge

1. Man was made in whose image?

2. Who said that it is more blessed to give than it is to receive?

3. What two things must we follow in order to see the Lord?

4. How do standards help a believer to identify with Christ?

5. List the five sources of standards as given in the chapter.

6. Name two examples given in the chapter illustrating specific instances where the Spirit of God served to set a standard.

7. Are standards set by tradition worthy of our consideration?

8. When a person sets individual standards for himself, should he seek to make them universal?

9. We are not to be legalistic. Standards do not save us. Standards are not an end in themselves. With this being the case, are standards necessary?

10. What place does the Sermon on the Mount hold in our understanding of standards?

Apply Your Knowledge

In evaluating your lifestyle, you would be wise to compare it to the Bible pattern of the Sermon on the Mount. Do you come up to the lofty standard set by Christ? If not, make a concentrated effort to possess the mind of Christ at all times. Having the mind of Christ and the Holy Spirit of Christ will enable you to live an overcoming life.

Expand Your Knowledge

The following books can enrich your understanding of the Pentecostal lifestyle. They can be ordered from the Pentecostal Publishing House.

• *Why? A Study of Christian Standards* (Word Aflame Publications).

• *In Search of Holiness* by David K. Bernard (Word Aflame Press).

• *Practical Holiness, A Second Look* by David K. Bernard (Word Aflame Press).

• *I Will Not Bow* by Nan M. Pamer (Word Aflame Press).

• *Modesty* by Nan M. Pamer (Word Aflame Press).

The Work of the Holy Ghost

8

> *And they went forth, and preached every where, the Lord working with them, and confirming the word with signs following. Amen.*
> *Mark 16:20*

Start with the Scriptures

Mark 16:17-18   I Corinthians 12
Acts 2:1-4

A Supernatural Church

There can be no question about the supernatural nature of the New Testament church.

Among His last words to His disciples, Jesus said, "And these signs shall follow them that believe; in my name shall they cast out devils; they shall speak with new tongues; they shall take up serpents; and if they drink any deadly thing, it shall not hurt them; they shall lay hands on the sick, and they shall recover" (Mark 16:17-18).

This was indeed a way of life with the early believers. The church was born with a supernatural experience as some 120 were filled with the Holy Ghost and spoke in languages they had never learned (Acts 2:1-4).

Many wonders and signs were done by the apostles (Acts 2:43). While the details of only a few of them are recorded in Scripture, enough of the record is preserved to show how the Lord worked with them, confirming the Word with signs following (Mark 16:20).

These supernatural signs seemed to serve two basic purposes: first, they ordinarily helped hurting people; second, they dramatically drew the attention of people to the claims of Christ.

After the lame man at the Temple gate called Beautiful was healed through the ministry of Peter and John, "All the people ran together unto them in the porch that is called Solomon's, greatly wondering" (Acts 3:11). This provided Peter an opportunity to preach Jesus.

Following the dramatic deaths of Ananias and Sapphira, "Great fear came upon all the church, and upon as many as heard these things" (Acts 5:11).

"And by the hands of the apostles were many signs and wonders wrought among the people; (and they were all with one accord in Solomon's porch. And of the rest durst no man join himself to them: but the people magnified them. And believers were the more added to the Lord, multitudes both of men and women)" (Acts 5:12-14).

Here is seen a common response to the miraculous: Those who choose not to believe and obey are made aware of the supernatural nature of the work of God, and they carefully avoid it. But those who choose to believe are strengthened and encouraged by the manifestation of the power of God.

Signs and Wonders in the New Testament

References to signs and wonders are common from the Day of Pentecost forward. In his first message, Peter said that Jesus of Nazareth was "a man approved of God among you by miracles and wonders and signs, which God did by him in the midst of you, as ye yourselves also know" (Acts 2:22).

Following the Day of Pentecost, one of the contributing factors to the growth of the church was the fact that "many wonders and signs were done by the apostles" (Acts 2:43).

When the early church was persecuted and commanded not to speak or teach in the name of Jesus, they prayed, "And now, Lord, behold their threatenings: and grant unto thy servants, that with all boldness they may speak thy word, by stretching forth thine hand to heal; and that signs and wonders may be done by the name of thy holy child Jesus" (Acts 4:29-30). Boldness did come to them, and after the dramatic deaths of Ananias and Sapphira, the apostles were involved in working "many signs and wonders" (Acts 5:12).

Paul and Barnabas abode a long time in Iconium "speaking boldly in the Lord" and working with signs and wonders (Acts 14:3). To the church at Rome, Paul described his ministry as one characterized by the miraculous (Romans 15:19). He made a similar claim to the Corinthians. (See II Corinthians 12:12.)

The role of signs and wonders in the confirmation of truth is seen in Hebrews 2:3-4: "How shall we escape, if we neglect so great salvation; which at the first began to be spoken by the Lord, and was confirmed unto us by them that heard him; God also bearing them witness, both with signs and wonders, and with divers miracles, and gifts of the Holy Ghost, according to his own will?"

When the nobleman whose son was at the point of death in Capernaum asked Jesus to heal his son, Jesus answered, "Except ye see signs and wonders, ye will not believe" (John 4:48). Some have thought Jesus' statement to be a rebuke, but it seems better to understand it as a simple statement of fact. Jesus did, after all, proceed to heal the boy. Jesus recognized that, in addition to the very real help they give to hurting people, signs and wonders are a great aid to faith.

Indeed, John, explaining the purpose behind the Gospel he wrote, said, "And many other signs truly did Jesus in the presence of his disciples, which are not written in this book: but these are written, that ye might believe that Jesus is the Christ, the Son of God; and that believing ye might have life through his name" (John 20:30-31).

Satan has a counterfeit to the miracle-working power of God, and as a result there will be false signs and wonders. (See Matthew 24:24; Mark 13:22; II Thessalonians 2:9.) But the sincere Christian who allows the Bible to be his final authority, who confesses the absolute deity of Jesus Christ, and whose interest in signs and wonders is to bring glory to the true God and to minister to those in need, does not have to fear the spurious.

The Work of the Holy Ghost in the Church Today

There is no indication in Scripture that God planned for the supernatural manifestation of His Spirit to cease during the church age. Instead, it is evident that His plan was for Christians to continue to do the work of God with the supernatural tools He placed in the church.

For example, Jesus said, "He that believeth on me, the works that I do shall he do also; and greater works than these shall he do; because I go unto my Father. And whatsoever ye shall ask in my name, that will I do, that the Father may be glorified in the

Son. If ye shall ask any thing in my name, I will do it" (John 14:12-14).

Jesus also pointed to the supernatural signs that follow believers (Mark 1:17-18). The most evident way supernatural ministry is performed is by means of the gifts of the Spirit discussed in detail in I Corinthians 12-14.

While the church at Corinth had many problems, they did not come behind in any gift (I Corinthians 1:7). The gifts of the Spirit operated profusely among them in spite of their abuse of them. In his letter Paul wrote to correct the use of the gifts, not to eliminate them.

The carnality of the Corinthians (I Corinthians 3:1-4) did not prevent the gifts from operating because the gifts of the Spirit are just that: *gifts*. They are not the evidence of spiritual maturity. They do not indicate that the person operating them has achieved advanced spiritual power. This is the difference between *gifts* and *fruit*. The fruit of the Spirit (Galatians 5:22-23) gives evidence of spiritual maturity. The fruit tells us something about the person's character and spirituality. But the gifts tell us nothing about the person's character or spirituality. Instead, they tell us about the nature of the giver, who is God Himself.

Many people confuse the distinction between the fruit of the Spirit and gifts of the Spirit. They think the gifts of the Spirit can operate only in the life of one who is spiritually mature, of sterling character, and perfect in every way. When, in their view, genuine gifts do operate through a person, they tend to idolize that individual as one who is far advanced spiritually. They seem to think spiritual gifts can operate only through those who are exceptional; they have little hope they could ever reach the place in God where He could trust them with these gifts.

But the Corinthians themselves are proof that the possession of gifts is not to be equated with maturity or perfection.

The validity of a gift is not so much determined by an examination of the life of the person through whom it operates. It is determined by comparing its message with the Word of God and its fruit with the criteria of edification, exhortation, and comfort (I Corinthians 14:3, 12).

The Nine Spiritual Gifts

While it is beyond the scope of this chapter to offer detailed teaching on the operation of all nine gifts of the Spirit listed in I Corinthians 12, a brief overview is in order.

For the sake of identification, these spiritual gifts are often divided into three groups of three:

The revelation gifts.
- Word of wisdom
- Word of knowledge
- Discerning of spirits

The power gifts.
- Faith
- Gifts of healings
- Working of miracles

The vocal gifts.
- Tongues
- Interpretation
- Prophecy

While the above organization of the spiritual gifts is helpful in identifying something of the nature of each gift and in remembering them, it is also somewhat artificial. The person who begins to operate in the spiritual gifts will soon discover that in practical operation various gifts will work together to accomplish common purposes. For example, a person operating with the gifts of healings may discover that the word of knowledge works in conjunction with that gift, giving him information about the sick person's condition. After healing has been ministered, he may find the word of wisdom in operation to give the healed individual direction as to how to conduct his life in a more spiritual or healthful manner.

It is important to know that the operation of the gifts are not to be taken as infallible. They are subject to the Bible, can be judged by the saints, and are under the authority of the ministry in the church. The Bible teaches us that the spirit of the prophet is subject to the prophet; that is, the gifts are channeled through Christians who are not perfect and who may fail to accurately reflect what God is saying and doing among His people. We should not be critical or doubters, but we are to act wisely and scripturally in the operation of spiritual gifts.

In our limited space, we will offer a few brief comments on each of the nine spiritual gifts. (Suggestions for additional study will be found under Expand Your Knowledge.)

The gift of the word of wisdom. This is not the "gift of wisdom"; it is the gift of the *word* of wisdom. Any believer may apply himself to the pursuit of wisdom and gain valuable progress (Proverbs 3:13-20; 4:5-13). He may pray and ask God for wisdom (James 1:5). But such wisdom is not the supernatural gift of the word of wisdom.

The gift of the word of wisdom may be defined as "a small portion (a word) of God's total wisdom supernaturally imparted by the Holy Spirit."

We must distinguish between "wisdom" and "knowledge." Knowledge is information. Wisdom is knowing what to do with that information. (See Ecclesiastes 10:10.)

The gift of the word of knowledge. Like the gift of the *word* of wisdom, this is the gift of the *word* of knowledge. It is not the "gift of knowledge." An individual can gain knowledge by study and research. He can gain great knowledge of the Scriptures. But this knowledge is not the supernatural gift of the word of knowledge.

The word of knowledge is information about which the believer has no personal knowledge but which is imparted to him by the Holy Ghost. The word of knowledge is a small portion of the total knowledge of God supernaturally imparted by the Holy Spirit.

The gift of discerning of spirits. This gift is sometimes mistakenly identified as the gift of "discernment." It seems that those who so identify it have it confused with the gift of the word of knowledge. Actually, it is the gift of discerning of *spirits*.

The word *discern* means "to recognize and distinguish between." The person being used in this gift will discern or recognize what spirits are at work in a given situation. There are several categories of spirits in existence:

- The Holy Spirit
- Faithful angels (Hebrews 1:13-14)
- Fallen angels
- Demons or evil spirits
- Human spirits

The gift of faith. There are three kinds of faith in the New Testament:

- The faith that comes by hearing the Word of God (Romans 10:17)
- The faith that is a part of the fruit of the Holy Spirit (Galatians 5:22)
- The gift of faith

The gift of faith is a small portion of the total faith of God, which is the gift of the Holy Spirit.

This gift may be operated in two ways:

- A person can exercise faith before God on behalf of a person, object, or situation (I Kings 17:1; 18:41-45; James 5:16-18).

- A person can exercise faith before a person, object, or situation on behalf of God (Joshua 10:12-13; Mark 11:12-14, 20-24; Matthew 17:20).

The gifts of healings. While there are similarities between healings and miracles in many cases, there are also important differences. A healing many times occurs gradually, almost imperceptibly, relieving the body of disease. A miracle, on the other hand, is usually instantaneous, usually perceptible, and may go beyond healing.

This spiritual gift is actually the *gifts* (plural) of *healings* (plural) (I Corinthians 12:28). This is important to recognize, for it reveals multiple acts of healing given by God through spiritually sensitive individuals as the needs are known.

The gift of the working of miracles. Miracles go beyond healings. They may involve the replacement of a bodily part which is missing or a visible and almost instantaneous change in some bodily part. Of course, a miracle may not involve a human body at all. It may involve an object, like the tree Jesus cursed or the sun and moon Joshua commanded to stand still, or it may pertain to a situation that is in need of divine intervention.

Basically, miracles are works contrary to nature. They are the accomplishments of the "impossible." They involve sudden reversals of the order to which we are accustomed.

The gift of prophecy. It is important to recognize the difference between the ministry of the prophet and the person who operates in the gift of prophecy. Prophets will exercise the gift of prophecy, but not everyone through whom the gift of prophecy operates is a prophet.

The gift of prophecy is a brief supernatural manifestation rather than involving every aspect of a person's ministry. Character is not involved; it is a gift. Prophecy is the act of prophesying (I Corinthians 14:31).

Prophecy is the speaking in a person's own language words given by the Holy Spirit.

Like all of the vocal gifts, the gift of prophecy is in some measure placed under the control of the believer. There are therefore regulations given by Paul as to their proper use (I Corinthians 14:1-33).

Prophecy is to be used for three purposes (I Corinthians 14:3):

- Edification
- Exhortation
- Comfort

The gift of divers kinds of tongues. The gift of divers kinds of tongues, while similar or the same in sound, is not to be confused with the speaking with tongues that occurs as the initial evidence of the baptism of the Holy Ghost. The gift of divers kinds of tongues and the manifestation of tongues as a person receives the Spirit are the same in essence but different in purpose and function. Just because a person speaks in tongues when he receives the Holy Ghost does not mean that he has received the gift of divers kinds of tongues.

Distinctions between the tongues in which a person speaks when receiving the Holy Spirit and the gift of divers kinds of tongues can be seen from a study of the experiences in the Bible.

• The Holy Spirit is for all people (Acts 2:39; 5:32; John 3:5; I Corinthians 12:13). The gift of divers kinds of tongues is not exercised by all (I Corinthians 12:11, 28, 30).

• The speaking with tongues in Acts 2, 10, and 19 does not fit the order of I Corinthians 14:27. Acts 2 is God's pattern for those initially receiving the gift of the Holy Spirit; I Corinthians 14:27 is God's pattern for those who, having previously been Spirit filled, operate the gift of divers kinds of tongues. The gift of divers kinds of tongues is to be operated by one person at a time, in order, and there is to be an interpretation. In Acts 2, 10, and 19, all believers spoke with tongues at once and no one interpreted.

We should not suppose, however, that the Spirit-filled person is not to speak in tongues unless an interpretation is given. On the contrary, in his private devotions, either alone or in the company of other worshipers, he may pray in an unknown tongue to God, and by this he edifies himself spiritually. But if he speaks with unction in a loud voice in a church service, he should then wait for an interpretation, either by himself or by someone else. If there is no interpretation, then he should not disturb the service again by speaking in tongues at that time.

The gift of divers kinds of tongues is the unction given to a believer by the Holy Spirit to speak in languages not understood by the speaker.

The gift of the interpretation of tongues. The gift of the interpretation of tongues is the anointing given by the Holy Spirit to speak in a language understood by the speaker the meaning of words previously spoken in a language he did not know.

It is important to realize that this is the gift of *interpretation* of tongues, not the gift of *translation* of tongues. This simple truth will help remove much skepticism concerning the operation of this gift.

The gift of divers kinds of tongues coupled with the interpretation of tongues is equivalent to prophecy (I Corinthians 14:5).

The interpretation of tongues is for the edification of the church (I Corinthians 14:26).

Summary

When people believe God for signs and wonders, they will not be disappointed. One of the things that distinguishes the true church from those who merely profess Christ is the confirmation of the Word of God with signs following (Mark 16:20).

Test Your Knowledge

1. What supernatural experience occurred at the birth of the church?
2. What are the two basic purposes of supernatural signs?
3. List the nine spiritual gifts and discuss their arrangement in categories.

Apply Your Knowledge

Since Paul said we are to "covet earnestly the best gifts" and to "desire spiritual gifts" (I Corinthians 12:31; 14:1), ask yourself, "What spiritual gift or gifts do I desire?" If God has given you the desire, He will give you the unction to use that particular gift.

Expand Your Knowledge

You may wish to consider the following books for further study on the spritual gifts:

- *The Gifts of the Spirit* by Lee Stoneking.
- *Spiritual Gifts* by David K. Bernard (Word Aflame Press).

These books are available from the Pentecostal Publishing House.

The Local Church 9

Not forsaking the assembling of ourselves together, as the manner of some is; but exhorting one another: and so much the more, as ye see the day approaching.

Hebrews 10:25

Local Churches in the Bible

The custom of Christians congregating in local assemblies for the purpose of worship is biblical. Before the birth of the church, the Jews formed the local synagogue for the purpose of being able to congregate. By the time of Christ, Jewish synagogues were located throughout the Mediterranean world.

The birth of the church took place in Jerusalem, and for a brief period the Jerusalem church was the only assembly. It was evident that this was not the will of God, and God permitted persecution to scatter the Christians. Everywhere they went they preached the gospel, and local assemblies were established. By the end of the first century, there were churches established throughout the Roman Empire.

Many of the epistles were addressed to local assemblies in various cities. In the second and third chapters of Revelation, we read the letters addressed to the seven churches of Asia. These were all local assemblies that had been established under Paul's ministry. The apostle wrote an epistle to the Colossians, revealing that an eighth assembly was also in the area.

From the time of the early church until now it has been convenient for Christians to gather in local congregations for the purpose of worship, inspiration, Bible study, and evangelism. It is no different with the United Pentecostal Church. The members of the United Pentecostal Church International assemble in local churches around the world. Sometimes these churches are small in number, and sometimes they consist of several hundred Christians.

Only One Church

Although Christians meet in local churches, there is only one church regardless of the historical and geographical setting. Time and place do not change the church.

"There is one body, and one Spirit, even as ye are called in one hope of your calling" (Ephesians 4:4).

"For by one Spirit are we all baptized into one body, whether we be Jews or Gentiles, whether we be bond or free; and have been all made to drink into one Spirit" (I Corinthians 12:13).

Since this one church is dispersed around the world and exists in the form of thousands of local assemblies, each assembly is a replica of the whole and is the entire church in miniature.

In the UPCI the local assembly is autonomous. The assembly may be incorporated in the state or nation in which it is located; it has the power to buy, sell, and possess real estate according to its local government and bylaws. The assembly maintains the church property and controls all matters relating to the physical nature of the assembly. The assembly has a roll of church membership, and from this are selected and appointed all church officials.

Being self-governing, the assembly is permitted the choice of selecting the form of local church government as suggested in the manual of the parent body; or it may adopt its own constitution, providing it does not conflict with the one given in the manual.

Being autonomous, the local assembly is not only self-governing, but also self-supporting and self-propagating. While the local church enjoys its privileges and freedom, it remains an integral part of the parent organization, the United Pentecostal Church International. The parent organization unites and fosters a spirit of togetherness throughout the body. Any spirit of independence is discouraged. Instead, all the local churches are to unite in a spirit of interdependence, contributing to the health and welfare of the whole.

Local Church Government

The form of local church government recognized in the UPCI is known as congregational, but the spiritual authority and material oversight is vested in the ministry. In this sense the government could be referred to as a theocracy—the rule of God through God-chosen and ordained men. The local assembly has the power and authority in selecting and calling a minister to pastor the church, but once the pastor is installed by the district superintendent, he is recognized as being God's shepherd in the church. A board of elders or deacons is often commissioned to serve with the pastor and under his leadership, but the pastor is charged with the responsibility to "feed the flock of God" and to take the oversight of all matters in the local assembly. He is the spiritual shepherd of the flock.

An Integral Part of the Parent Church

Although the local assembly is wholly autonomous in nature, yet the pastor and local ministers are an integral part of the international body. Moreover, the church may be affiliated with the international fellowship, and it is involved with all of the various cooperative efforts of the district and international organization. There are three main areas where this interdependence is accomplished.

The pastor holds credentials with the United Pentecostal Church International. The fellowship of the United Pentecostal Church is primarily on the ministerial level. If the pastor is a licensed minister of the parent body, the assembly, although it may not be affiliated, is accepted as being a part of the organization. In other words the parent body accepts and fellowships the members of the local assembly on the basis that the pastor is a minister in the UPCI.

The Articles of Faith of the United Pentecostal Church International are accepted by each United Pentecostal Church.

A local assembly is only as strong as the doctrines that are taught and preached over the pulpit. Truth and holiness are the two factors that not only identify any assembly but also give that church power and strength to fulfill God's plan for its existence.

Because of this, the UPCI has adopted a statement of biblical truth known as the Articles of Faith. As a part of the fellowship in the UPCI, the local assembly accepts and acknowledges its belief in the Articles of Faith.

Certainly the Bible is recognized as the final authority upon all spiritual and eternal matters. In every United Pentecostal church pulpit the Word of God is honored and proclaimed to be infallible, the message of eternal life, to be believed and obeyed. Moreover, the United Pentecostal Church does not accept any other authority for doctrine and faith, not even its Articles of Faith. The Articles of Faith are merely guidelines for fellowship and do not have the same authority as Scripture.

Since the Articles of Faith are guidelines for fellowship, any local assembly that refuses to accept the Articles of Faith will not be identified with the international body. It is this statement of faith and standards that identifies all United Pentecostal churches.

Affiliation offers protection to every local assembly. It is strongly recommended that every local assembly affiliate with the parent body. This affiliation is not mandatory and remains optional, but it offers the congregation protection since it comes under the umbrella of legal recognized privileges of the parent church. By affiliating, the local church does not lose its autonomous power but it gains legal recognition and protection. In difficult circumstances and when problems arise, the affiliated church is able legally to call upon the parent church for assistance and guidance.

A Spiritual Home

A home has greater significance than being just a house where people reside. If it is only an address a person needs, he can rent a post office box. But in everyone's heart resides a longing for a place of rest, security, and belonging. A person's home gives him identity, offers an environment where he can relax, and provides emotional and spiritual shelter from the storms of life.

Christians need more than just an earthly home, however. They also need a spiritual home, a sanctuary where they can experience the joy of worship, find comfort among other believers, learn the Word of God and be inspired with new faith and courage. The local church provides such a spiritual home for believers who attend a United Pentecostal church.

Christians in their spiritual home grow to be stable, steadfast believers. They receive wise direction for their lives and develop an abiding trust in God. On the other hand, professing Christians who have no church home often drift from church to church. Without roots, they may soon become spiritual tramps with no place to call their own.

It is such places of worship that the apostle had in mind when he exhorted the Hebrews to not forsake their church attendance. "Not forsaking the assembling of ourselves together, as the manner of some is; but exhorting one another: and so much the more, as ye see the day approaching" (Hebrews 10:25).

The United Pentecostal Church Home Becomes Many Things to the Christian

The local church is the Christian's birthplace. It is understood that God is no respecter of place, and He gives His Spirit to believers in many different settings. People have been known to receive the Holy

Ghost riding in automobiles, traveling by train, in the open field, at home, and at work. Most believers, however, receive their Pentecostal experience in the local church. It is at church where they most likely hear the gospel preached and are won to the Lord. Generally it is also in the local church where they are baptized in water.

Most sinners repent at the altars of the local church, and at repentance and water baptism the burdens of sin are lifted. Even those saints of God who receive the Holy Ghost in places other than at the local church look to the local church as their birthplace. From a local assembly the message of salvation came to them, creating faith that led to being born again and the beginning of a new life.

The local church is the center of studying God's Word. Every healthy assembly is rooted and grounded in the Word of God. The Bible is the source of faith. "So then faith cometh by hearing, and hearing by the word of God" (Romans 10:17).

God's Word is truth and a powerful agent for sanctification. All United Pentecostal churches are Bible-believing churches. As such, their focus is Bible teaching and this focus results in strong congregations standing for truth and a holy lifestyle.

The local church is the center for worship. Everywhere God is seeking men and women to worship Him in spirit and in truth. (See John 4:24.) Worship that is acceptable to God contains two elements: truth and spirit.

The UPCI proclaims the truth in the knowledge of God. They know whom they worship. Without the knowledge of the one true God, it is impossible to worship in truth. Over the pulpits of the United Pentecostal local churches is proclaimed the revelation of God in Jesus Christ.

True worship is essential for personal Christian growth and effective evangelistic outreach. Therefore, the local assembly must strive to be full of life and power—the life and power of the Holy Spirit. The local assembly of the UPCI is not satisfied with ritualistic worship, but rather it seeks a vibrating anointing and a fresh flow of Holy Ghost power.

The local church is the center of fellowship. Every Christian needs fellowship. The United Pentecostal Church is basically concerned with ministering to man's needs, both spiritual and natural. Thus the ministry of the church is not limited to the spiritual needs, but it seeks to help each person to fulfill his physical, social, mental, and emotional needs. He needs Christian fellowship, for through communication and sharing with fellow Christians he will discover the answers that will enable him to grow into a mature, healthy Christian.

In the local UPCI church many activities bring Christians together. Weddings, anniversaries, and other special events in the life of a family take place in the church fellowship hall and within the church family. Dinners, banquets, and pleasant evenings are planned in an informal atmosphere. Upon such occasions the members relax and enjoy one another's company.

The United Pentecostal Church Provides a Healthy Relationship Between the Pastor and the Members

In the tenth chapter of the Gospel of John, Jesus taught that His disciples were sheep and that He was their Shepherd. This truth is taught many places in the Scriptures. The church is the sheepfold. The church members are sheep and Jesus is the Shepherd. Jesus Christ is the Chief Shepherd, and He has made the pastors undershepherds of local assemblies (I Peter 5:1-4).

The shepherd of the flock leads the sheep to pasture and watches over them while they feed. He protects them from wild animals that might destroy them. He watches over the sheep to see that they do not stray from the fold. He gives special loving care to the young lambs and weak ones. As the shepherd, he is their guide and provider.

Three times Jesus instructed Simon Peter to feed His lambs and His sheep. (See John 21:15-17.) Through the ministry of God's Word the pastor teaches and instructs the Christians. The Word of God is called both milk and strong meat.

The shepherd of the flock is not only the one who feeds, but he is also the one who leads. He never drives the sheep for they would simply scatter. Sheep are not driven, but they are led. In prayer, worship, fasting, dedication, and sacrifice, the shepherd leads the sheep. The sheep follow his leadership, for they have confidence in their pastor. They know his voice and trust him.

"My sheep hear my voice, and I know them, and they follow me" (John 10:27).

The Minister Ministers Within the Local Church

Jesus placed within His church a fivefold ministry: apostles, prophets, evangelists, pastors, and teachers (Ephesians 4:11).

The apostle Paul made it clear that the ministry's main work would be done within the church itself. He clearly stated the purpose of the fivefold ministry as being

- Perfecting the saints;
- Work of the ministry;
- Edifying the body of Christ.

In this same statement the apostle gave the goal towards which the ministry would be laboring. The objective of the ministry is to bring the Christians to

- Unity of the faith;
- Knowledge of Jesus Christ;
- Perfection;
- Christ-likeness;
- Spiritual maturity.

As the ministry succeeds in this God-ordained purpose, the church becomes a healthy body with every member of the body actively functioning in the spirit of love. Such a church experiences revival, growth, and expansion.

An Active Christian Is a Happy Christian

The local assembly provides many avenues of profitable service and ministry for every Christian. This creates an atmosphere where every member is a happy Christian. There is a sense of fulfillment in his Christian walk.

Within the local assembly there is a wide range of responsibility and service:

- Administration: elders, deacons, trustees, departmental leaders.
- Departments: Sunday school, youth ministry, ladies ministry, outreach. Each of these departments needs a full staff.
- Music: choir and orchestra. This opens the door of ministry to many musicians and singers.
- Maintenance of Church Property: janitor, custodian and others.

The opportunity of service is not just confined to the four walls of the church building. Numerous ministries of outreach are promoted from the local assembly of the UPCI. Lay workers conduct regular meetings in rescue missions, hospitals, rest homes, and prisons. Whole neighborhoods are canvassed by knocking on doors and handing out gospel literature. Many members become actively involved in teaching home Bible studies.

There need be no idle member of the flock in any United Pentecostal church. Everyone can be busily engaged with his personal ministry, thus creating an atmosphere of happy fulfillment of the entire body.

The Local Church Becomes a Mother Church

Like mothers, local churches are to expand their family by establishing new assemblies. Not only are many new converts to be born at their altars, but many new assemblies must also come from each local church.

Many local churches have pioneered other assemblies. This is sometimes done through much personal sacrifice. The mother church gives up members and capable dedicated workers as well as financial offerings to create another local church in the area. It happens when the pastor and congregation have a vision and burden for the lost. The reward is the satisfaction of knowing that the church has developed and matured into a strong assembly and taken its place among the thousands of healthy United Pentecostal churches scattered around the world.

Test Your Knowledge

1. Write a clear definition of the following terms:
   • theocracy
   • autonomous

2. State the benefits for a local assembly being affiliated with the UPCI.

3. What is the Lord's purpose in placing within the church the fivefold ministry?

Apply Your Knowledge

With a greater knowledge of the structure and function of the local assembly, there will come a great appreciation for the function and activities of the local church. This may be shown by

- Expressing to your pastor your love and appreciation for him;
- Praying regularly for your pastor and all the leaders in the church.

Carefully consider the whole ministry of your local church. Are there some weak areas? Offer yourself to the Lord and then to your pastor as being willing to minister in these places of need.

Expand Your Knowledge

You may expand your knowledge by doing some research in these areas:

- Read and study the constitution of your local church.
- Make a complete list of all offices and staff members in the various departments of the church.
- Are there inactive members attending your local church? Study and locate areas where these people might find a ministry. Discuss this with your pastor.
- Study the history of the local church. Make a list of all ministers and missionaries who entered the ministry while members of this church.

Strength in Unity **10**

Behold, how good and how pleasant it is for
brethren to dwell together in unity!

Psalm 133:1

Start with the Scriptures

I Corinthians 1:10   Ephesians 4:3
II Corinthians 13:11   Philippians 3:16-17

Purpose

Inlaid in the terrazzo flooring of the foyer of the World Evangelism Center is the original motto of the United Pentecostal Church International: "The Whole Gospel to the Whole World."

This purpose can best be accomplished by men and women uniting together for a common cause. It is this fact that gives reason for the UPCI to exist.

The new birth, and not church membership, makes an individual a member of the body of

Christ. In the visible church, strength comes from unity; by a cooperative effort a group of people can accomplish its purpose.

Membership

Membership in the United Pentecostal Church International is made up of all ministers and missionaries who hold an accredited credential, and all members of local assemblies that are affiliated with the UPCI.

This organizational structure is not meant to be a master over its members, but a servant. It has been created to serve its constituents. In this role of servanthood, the UPCI has been significantly blessed. The preacher of Ecclesiastes said that "two are better than one; because they have a good reward for their labour. For if they fall, the one will lift up his fellow: but woe to him that is alone when he falleth; for he hath not another to help him up" (Ecclesiastes 4:9-10). Unity and a united effort are not to be despised, but appreciated. Many hands make the load light.

Organizational Structure

The affiliated local church, which maintains autonomy in the organizational structure, works in harmony with the other levels of organization. This church and its pastor form a complete entity in themselves. These local churches are self-supporting, self-governing, and self-propagating. But each assembly also blends its efforts and gifts with other assemblies for the purposes of fellowship and of evangelization of the world.

Local churches are joined together in geographical sections, with each section having a presbyter. This presbyter is normally elected at an annual sectional conference, along with other sectional officials.

The next level in the organizational structure is that of the district. The UPCI is divided into fifty-five districts, most of which are states or provinces. The sectional presbyters, along with the district superintendent and the district secretary/treasurer make up the District Board. All district officers (other than presbyters) are elected at an annual district conference.

The general level is next in the organizational structure. The general superintendent, the assistant general superintendents, the general secretary-treasurer, the director of Foreign Missions, the director of Home Missions, the editor in chief, the Sunday School director, the president of the General Youth Division, the superintendent of the Division of Education, a general executive presbyter for each region, a general presbyter from each zone, and a general presbyter for each district forms the Board of General Presbyters, known as the General Board.

As the highest board in the organization, the General Board meets twice annually to oversee the administration of the UPCI. (A smaller Executive Board, made up of members from the General Board, meets more often to take care of necessary official business.) All divisions, committees, and boards are subject to the oversight of the general conference, administered by the General Board, as defined by the manual of the organization.

World Evangelism Center

The purpose and function of the headquarters building of the UPCI is clearly defined by the name "World Evangelism Center." The work transacted within the building reaches around the world, as commissioned by the Lord.

Church Administration

Church Administration oversees the business and activities of World Evangelism Center and the UPCI. The general superintendent, the assistant general superintendents, and the general secretary-treasurer direct Church Administration. With the help of administrative assistants and staff, they seek to coordinate the activities of all divisions.

Church Administration plans the annual general conference of the UPCI. This conference in session is the ruling body and voice of the UPCI. Church Administration also plans and coordinates international conferences for the worldwide fellowship. International conferences are held every four or five years, usually in a foreign nation.

Church Administration maintains the ministerial and church records and processes all ministerial licenses. The general superintendent, or his delegated representative, oversees the election of officers at each district conference.

Church Administration directly oversees several areas of service at World Evangelism Center such as ministers' insurance, stewardship, information technology, and employee relations.

Another important segment of Church Administration is the Center for the Study of Oneness Pentecostalism. The Center collects, preserves, and displays historical materials dating back to the earliest days of the Pentecostal outpouring in the twentieth century.

The Pentecostal Historical Society enrolls members who share the value of the work of the Center. *Connect* is a newsletter that publicizes the work and progress of this body. The Center for the Study of Oneness Pentecostalism also sponsors the Feast of Pentecost Heritage Conference.

Divisions

The UPCI has chosen to divide its areas of responsibility into various divisions. Each division has been commissioned to various duties and arenas of accomplishment, but all the divisions work together to carry out the total commission of the church.

Division of Publications. The Division of Publications serves as the channel for publishing Bible-centered literature on behalf of the UPCI. In cooperation with the other divisions, the Division of Publications promotes evangelism through books, periodicals, tracts, Sunday school curriculum, and other printed matter.

The Division of Publications consists of five different departments. The officers of the Division of Publications are president (general superintendent), vice president (general secretary-treasurer), the editor in chief, the associate editor/editors, the Pentecostal Publishing House administrator, the editor and the associate editor of Word Aflame Sunday School Curriculum, the marketing director, and the editor of the *Pentecostal Herald.*

The Editorial Department is directed by the editor in chief, who serves as the editor in chief for the entire organization. He is assisted by an associate editor. The Editorial Department is responsible for the editing and publishing of the *Forward*, a magazine for ministers. It also approves all manuscripts for all other divisional periodicals and publications, including the Sunday school literature.

A Board of Publications meets twice annually to review and oversee the areas of publication of the organization. An Executive Publications Committee decides on the publication of all book and tract manuscripts.

The Herald Department is responsible for the editing and publishing of the *Pentecostal Herald* (the official organ). The Herald editor meets annually with a think tank of advisors to plan the content and direction of the magazine.

The department called the Pentecostal Publishing House exists for the purpose of spreading whole gospel to the whole world through the production and dissemination of religious knowledge, useful literature, and spiritual information in the form of books, tracts, periodicals, and other printed matter.

The Pentecostal Publishing House publishes books under the name Word Aflame Press. With over 260 titles currently in print, Word Aflame Press adds several books each year to its library.

Another strong arm of the Division of Publications is Word Aflame Publications. This department is responsible for producing Sunday school curriculum for all ages.

The Word Aflame curriculum is divided into eight age levels, each under the ultimate direction and oversight of the Curriculum Committee. (See Sunday School Division later in this chapter.) Field editors for each level from Toddler through Adult are responsible for developing and editing their respective levels. The work of the field editors of the first five levels, Toddler through PreTeen, is supervised and coordinated by the children's editor. The associate editor of Word Aflame oversees the work of the field editors of the Teen and Youth levels. The editor of Word Aflame oversees the Adult level and directs the production of all other levels.

Word Aflame Publications has also developed an undated elective series of curriculum materials. The elective series library has a growing number of titles. Groups such as youth, college/career, families senior citizens, new converts, singles, and dating couples have material designed especially for them.

The Marketing Department is responsible for the marketing of all of the products of the Division of Publications, as well as any products of other divisions when requested by those divisions.

Division of Education. The purpose of the Division of Education is to preserve apostolic doctrine, experience, and practice in the educational systems of the UPCI.

The Division of Education currently endorses seven Bible colleges and one graduate school. The following is a list of these institutions:

- Apostolic Bible Institute—St. Paul, MN *(apostolic.org)*
- Centro Teologico Ministerial—Channelview, TX *(centroteologico.net)*
- Christian Life College—Stockton, CA *(clc.edu)*
- Gateway College of Evangelism—Florissant, MO *(gatewaycollege.net)*
- Indiana Bible College—Indianapolis, IN *(indianabiblecollege.org)*
- Northeast Christian College—Fredericton, NB, *(northeastchristiancollege.com)*
- Texas Bible College—Houston, TX *(texasbiblecollege.com)*
- Urshan Graduate School of Theology—Hazelwood, MO *(ugst.org)*

The Urshan Graduate School of Theology is owned and operated by the UPCI and is governed by its own school board. It offers the master of theological studies degree and the master of divinity degree. It is designed to qualify people for pastoral and evangelistic ministries, as Bible college instructors, as theological writers, and as military or prison chaplains. Founded in 2000, with its first classes in 2001, the school is working toward accreditation with the Association of Theological Schools.

The Division of Education acts in an advisory capacity to its more than 600 Christian schools and home schools. It also provides a structure for the Association of Christian Teachers and Schools (ACTS). This association provides student conventions, teachers' conferences, doctrinal study resources, and the ACTS Student Honor Society.

The superintendent of education, the secretary of education, and three other ministers make up the

Board of Education. These officers are appointed by the General Board and ratified by the general conference.

The division of education serves as the endorsing division for the placement of chaplains within the military. Several chaplains serve in the military at this time, with more in training.

Foreign Missions Division. See chapter 12.

Home Missions Division. See chapter 11.

Media Missions Division. With deep conviction that the gospel of the Lord Jesus Christ must be preached to all people, and sensing the urgency of this hour and the opportunity offered by information technology to minister to more people for each dollar invested, the UPCI established the Media Missions Division to "Reach every nation with Bible salvation, true Bible salvation that saves from sin."

Guided by a director, an assistant to the director, a secretary, and six regional commissioners as well as a director from each of the districts of the UPCI, Media Missions Division produces programs that are heard via radio and the Internet *(www.thereishopefor-today.com* and *www.myhoperadio.com*).

The main financial support of the Media Missions Division is the Mission of Hope offering, received in North America on the Sunday before Thanksgiving. It is the division's hope to partner with churches and individuals to bring "Biblical answers to real life questions."

Youth Division. The mission of the General Youth Division is to serve the local churches of the UPCI, assisting them in fulfilling the great commission given by Jesus Christ, which is to evangelize the lost and disciple the converted.

The General Youth Division has three general officers: the general president, the general secretary, and the director of promotion. These officers give their full time and attention to the development and direction of the youth activities of the fellowship.

Each district also has a youth president and youth secretary. The district youth presidents join with the general officers to form the General Youth Committee.

The General Youth Division is involved in several ministries including Apostolic Youth Corps, Bible Quizzing, Campus Ministry, Uplink: A Day of Prayer and Fasting, Bible College Scholarships, Youth Week, North American Youth Congress, and The Commune-ity. This division publishes a variety of resources including Youth home Bible studies, *Insideout* magazine, and a moral purity curriculum entitled "Worth the Wait."

Since 1952, the General Youth Division has received an annual Sheaves for Christ offering. To raise funds for this offering, young people of the local churches are involved in various fundraising efforts. The Sheaves for Christ funds bless a variety of ministries. Foreign Missions, Home Missions, Media Missions, the Division of Education, Tupelo Children's Mansion, Lighthouse Ranch for Boys, and Spirit of Freedom Ministries are among those who annually receive support from Sheaves for Christ.

Sunday School Division. The General Sunday School Division is a valuable part of the UPCI. In training members of local churches, Sunday school provides Christian education for thousands of people.

The officers of the Sunday School Division are a general Sunday school director, a general Sunday school secretary, and a director of promotions. These officers are responsible for the oversight and direction of this division.

Officers are elected on the district and sectional levels as well. The district Sunday school directors serve on the General Sunday School Board with the general officers and the editor and the associate editor of Word Aflame Publications.

The general Sunday school director serves as chairman of the Literature Curriculum Development Committee. This committee consists of the chairman, ten members appointed by the General Board, the editor in chief, and the editor and the associate editor of Word Aflame literature. This committee is responsible for the development of curriculum and the constant revisions required to keep the curriculum fresh and useful.

Many ministries and resources are under the Sunday School Division oversight:

- Teacher training and certification
- Children's Ministry Association
- Children's Ministry Convention
- Children's Prayer Revival
- Junior Bible Quizzing
- Junior camps
- Scouting
- Singles ministry
- *Christian Educator* magazine
- Devotional resources (B.R.E.A.D.)
- Outreach tools (C.A.R.E. and H.O.P.E.)
- Kids Power Up radio program

The General Sunday School Division receives an annual Save Our Children offering, beginning on January 15 and concluding on Easter Sunday. This offering funds various programs as well as other needs at home and on the foreign field.

Ladies Ministries. The organization created the Ladies Ministries for the purpose of aiding and assisting all levels of ministry in the UPCI as directed by the General Board and general conference.

The Ladies Ministries' annual Mothers Memorial offering centers around Mother's Day in May. The money funds Ladies Ministries Connections, Foreign Missions, Home Missions, Lighthouse Ranch for Boys, Division of Education, Media Missions, World Network of Prayer, New Beginnings, Tupelo Children's Mansion, Spirit of Freedom Ministries, and Urshan Graduate School of Theology.

With two general officers—a president and a secretary—and district presidents, the ladies continue to be an immense blessing to the UPCI.

Endorsed Projects

Along with the seven endorsed Bible colleges and one graduate school, there are six other endorsed projects of the United Pentecostal Church International.

Tupelo Children's Mansion. Located in Tupelo, Mississippi *(tcmm.org)*, this is a children's home for children without parents and children with troubled family situations.

The Lighthouse Ranch for Boys. Located in Loranger, Louisiana *(lighthouseranch.com)*, this home has been a help to many troubled young boys who needed a second chance.

The Spirit of Freedom Ministries. Located in Metairie, Louisiana *(sofm.org)*, this is a ministry directed at helping those with alcohol and drug problems.

New Beginnings International Children's and Family Services. Located in Tupelo, Mississippi *(NewBeginningsAdoptions.com)*, New Beginnings promotes "LIFE" for the unborn child, "HOPE" for birthmothers, and "forever families" for children through a variety of ministry programs.

Pentecostal Minister training Network. Located in Pearland, Texas *(pcminister.com)*, this endorsed ministry offers online training for churches and ministers.

Great Lakes University. Located in Auburn Hills, Michigan (*gluniv.org*), this is a liberal arts college.

These projects extend the efforts of the UPCI to needy fields.

Conclusion

There is strength in unity. "A threefold cord is not quickly broken" (Ecclesiastes 4:12). This biblical advice points to the wisdom of unity. Through the unified efforts of the UPCI, the motto "The Whole Gospel to the Whole World" is becoming a reality.

Test Your Knowledge

1. What are the four levels of the structure of the UPCI?
2. How many Bible colleges are endorsed by the UPCI?
3. What is the highest ruling voice in the UPCI?
4. List at least four divisions.
5. Are the local churches autonomous?

Apply Your Knowledge

With your new understanding of the UPCI, make the work of each division, each project, each program, and all the personnel at World Evangelism Center a part of your prayerful interest.

Expand Your Knowledge

For further information regarding any division, contact that division directly at the World Evangelism Center, 8855 Dunn Road, Hazelwood, Missouri 63042-2299. You can also access each division at *upci.org.*

A Church in Every Community

11

And as they went through the cities, they delivered them the decrees for to keep, that were ordained of the apostles and elders which were at Jerusalem. And so were the churches established in the faith, and increased in number daily.

Acts 16:4-5

Start with the Scriptures

Matthew 28:18-20   Acts 10; 16; 19:10

The General Home Missions Division, shouldering the responsibility of evangelizing North America (United States and Canada), is effective only by the uniting of the churches of the United Pentecostal Church International for this worthy cause. By adding the structure of organization to collective resources and burdens, the seemingly impossible task of evangelizing every province, state, city, and person in North America can be accomplished.

The Home Missions Division consists of a general director, a general secretary, director of Multicultural Ministries, director of Metro Evangelism, director of Promotions and Publications, seven regional directors, a Board of Directors, an Administrative Committee, and a Planning Committee.

The Concept of Home Missions

Within the North American borders, a multitude of different cultures exist. Indeed, North America developed as the melting pot of the world, blending cultures, nationalities, and races together. The Home Missions Division is committed to reaching all the people of North America through every viable approach.

The planting (or starting) of churches is the top priority of the Home Missions Division. Every town, city, and village deserves a truth-proclaiming church, and metropolitan areas need many churches.

Accompanying the priority of starting churches, the Home Missions Division supports ways and means to promote church planting. An annual training seminar is conducted for all home missionaries, teaching effective approaches to starting a church.

Double-in-a-Decade (begun in 2004) is a burden of the Home Missions Division to see the number of United Pentecostal Churches double throughout North America in ten years. Along with pioneer church planters, we are seeing growth with the mother/daughter church planting program. This takes place when a mother church plants a new (daughter) congregation in an unevangelized community or culture. The mother church provides leadership, finances, and other areas of support when needed for the daughter congregation.

The division also offers tools for soulwinning and personal evangelism. Financial support is available to home missions efforts on the district and national levels for both personal livelihood and property grants. Tracts and literature are provided for missionaries at no cost.

Metro Evangelism is a specialized effort to reach the metropolitan areas, where the high costs of living and property hinder the start of churches. As a missions endeavor, a qualified metro missionary may travel to churches in an effort to raise monthly commitments for support. When he goes to his designated metropolitan area, he can then devote himself fully to the evangelism effort and to establishing a church.

Spanish Evangelism is the effort to evangelize the Hispanic community. As the fastest growing minority group in North America, Hispanics now number over thirty million people. The Home Missions Division sponsors leadership training sessions for Hispanic pastors, the production of Spanish literature including tracts, and general promotion of Hispanic evangelism. Numerous churches have Spanish outreaches, and many Spanish-speaking churches exist within the UPCI in North America. A ministry director, elected by the annual Spanish Evangelism Conference, serves with the Spanish Evangelism Board in leading this ministry under the direction of the Home Missions Division.

Evangelism of the Black community has seen dynamic growth over the years with an organized effort. This endeavor is centralized around a national conference, the annual Black Evangelism Conference, focusing on the need to reach the Black population and to offer training to those who are involved with Black evangelism. The number of delegates attending the conference has grown to a few thousand, and the effort has witnessed thousands of Blacks becoming members of United Pentecostal churches. A ministry director, elected by the annual

Black Evangelism Conference, serves with the Black Evangelism Board in leading this ministry under the direction of the Home Missions Division.

Prison Ministry is also flourishing under the care of Home Missions and its daughter organization, Christian Prisoner Fellowship (CPF). The lonely, incarcerated, lost souls locked behind prison bars deserve to feel the warm compassion of our loving Savior. Jesus specifically mentioned the need to evangelize the prisons in Matthew 25. The prison systems are searching for means of rehabilitation. The UPCI has stepped forward to be a part of the answer.

Christian Prisoner Fellowship has enlisted over 1,500 apostolic volunteer chaplains serving in every state and province. The goal of developing and maintaining a prison evangelistic effort in every institution in North America is being realized in several districts. The Home Missions Division produces many books and materials for prisoner discipleship.

The Life in Focus Education (LIFE) program has opened many doors, created phenomenal results, and helped people who suffer from drug addiction. LIFE has been formally approved in many states as an appropriate alternative to Alcoholics Anonymous and Narcotics Anonymous. Many people are being baptized in Jesus' name and filled with the Holy Ghost through the local church as a result of this program.

The Deaf Ministry of the UPCI has also witnessed marvelous growth in recent years. With one percent of this continent's population being deaf and about one out of ten people suffering from hearing impairment, evangelizing this community is a great responsibility. This awesome need has thrust the Home Missions Division into producing specialized literature and tracts, sponsoring specific promotions, and directing the coordination of the endeavor.

A deaf ministry coordinator leads the organizing of this endeavor with a priority focus on the Annual Deaf Camp Meeting and Workshop that attracts both deaf and hearing impaired individuals as well as interpreters for the deaf from across the continent. Specialized classes are conducted simultaneously daily with an evening rally culminating the daily activities. Each year deaf people receive the Holy Ghost in the meeting. The interest in this ministry continues to grow in our fellowship.

Multicultural Ministries is the endeavor to evangelize all ethnic groups within the United States and Canada. Chinese, Vietnamese, Laotian, other Asian, and European people are located in various communities in North America. Speaking their mother languages and maintaining their own cultures, these groups need someone to bring them the message of Bible salvation. It has been estimated that over 90 percent of the ethnic population within North America remains unevangelized by any Christian group. The Home Missions Division is now ministering to fifty-three language groups and sixty-nine cultures on a weekly basis.

Additional outreach endeavors of the Home Missions Division include Pentecost Sunday, Power Weekend, All Nations Sunday, and Holy Ghost Crusades across the United States and Canada.

Accompanying the various ministry endeavors, the Home Missions Division produces and provides materials for evangelism. Soulwinning tools (including *Exploring God's Word*), church growth and Bible study materials, tracts, and other evangelism tools are continually developed and distributed. In this way, the Home Missions Division serves the United Pentecostal Church International with helpful resources (*homemissionsdivision.com*).

The Need of Evangelism

In 1900, in North America one church existed for every 414 people. Today, one church exists for every 722 people. This means that twenty-four churches existed for every 10,000 people in 1900, and today only fourteen churches exist for every 10,000 people.

According to the Institute for American Church Growth, 75-80 percent of the churches in America have plateaued or are declining. Research indicates that a church will reach its peak attendance within the first fifteen years of its existence.

While North America's population has grown by 11.4 percent in the last ten years, church denominations have lost 2,765,000 members each year with 400 to 500 churches dying each year. Sunday school attendance has fallen 25 percent in the last ten years, producing an incredible 37 percent of adults without Bible training as a child (as compared to 6 percent of adults with no Bible training as a child in 1954). A grave famine of the Word of God has left a void, but remarkably, there is also a recognized hunger for God's Word among these same people.

What an hour for home missions! Fundamental, conservative churches are experiencing exceptional growth. The present-day church lives in the golden day of opportunity for evangelism and for establishing new churches.

The Need for New Churches

New churches and evangelism have been the lifeline of the United Pentecostal Church International. Over 10 percent of the United Pentecostal Church International population has perpetually existed under home missions status (churches five years old or less), and new souls and peoples are continually added in all the churches of the fellowship.

The starting of churches is the lifeline of any church organization. According to some studies, church denominations slipped into decline when they lost their focus and priority on church planting. At the same time, denominations that are growing maintain an impetus to start churches.

Giving a church to a community is among the greatest gifts. God greatly blesses the new mission as well as the churches that contribute toward its birth. New missions realize an increase in evangelism efficiency—younger churches report a higher percentage growth rate than older churches. In church growth terms, the younger churches grow better. In the endeavor to effectively evangelize a community, therefore, beginning new churches is more effective than attempting to become a "super-church."

According to studies at the Fuller Institute of Church Growth, the average person residing in North America possesses at least thirty-eight different "felt" needs (real or unreal needs) at any interval of life. These studies indicate that the largest church, even the most efficient evangelistic outreach center, is capable of ministering effectively to a maximum of only five to six of the "felt" needs in the community.

This limitation is understandable when we realize that every church possesses a personality that ministers only to certain segments of the community. The alternative to the concept of the "super-church" that will effectively minister to more community needs is to establish more churches. Two churches together, with alternative personalities, may effectively minister to eight, nine, or even ten of the "felt" needs of a community. With the increase in the number of churches, more of the community will be reached.

The smile of God over a home missions effort creates positive ripples around the world. Today

133

North America is the base for world evangelism, and the broadening of the base strengthens the means of reaching the world. By evangelizing North America, we produce both men and money to reach the world. (Financially speaking, some churches started under the Christmas for Christ banner can be found listed among the top contributors to the Foreign Missions Division of the United Pentecostal Church International.) Moreover, citizens of foreign countries, transformed by the Holy Ghost while in North America, return home to their native countries and deliver the gospel message of truth.

In the New Testament, a strong, vigorous effort to start churches everywhere can be seen in the missionary activities of the apostle Paul and others. They willingly made personal sacrifices in order to make the gospel available to all cities and communities. They exhibited a fervent desire to extend the kingdom of God to the ends of their world. From the biblical record, it is apparent that wherever converts were made a church was begun. Soulwinning and church planting fused into one effort. They allowed the results of evangelism to flow into the creation of a new church.

Home Missions Financial Support

Through the Metro Evangelism program, a home missionary visits churches to raise funds for his financial support during the time he is establishing a church in a metropolitan area. This is one method of funding the needs of Home Missions. The major support upon which the Home Missions Division depends, however, is the Christmas for Christ program.

The Christmas for Christ program provides churches and congregations a way to give to Jesus

Christ on His celebrated birthday—Christmas. In today's commercialized environment, the real meaning of Christmas often gently slips even from the hearts of believers. In harmony with the purpose for which Jesus was born, we celebrate His birth by giving gifts of our finances in an effort to reach lost souls with the gospel.

The Christmas for Christ program annually receives approximately $3 million, which is used to fund infant churches and home missionary pastors, provide evangelistic resources (including revivals) for new churches, train home missionary pastors, and support special ministries. These funds support the Home Missions endeavors to reach into hundreds of new areas each year, bringing the hope of the gospel to the unsaved.

The Church-in-a-Day program offers financial help to a growing congregation in need of a new facility for present and future growth. Under this program, finances are made available with an interest-free loan. The local church has 100 months to repay the program in order to help another congregation to build or to buy an existing building. This is a wonderful way to assist the home missionaries in planning for their future building needs.

The United Pentecostal Church International Youth Division, through Sheaves for Christ, provides property grants for new churches. Special care is required to sustain infant life. Likewise, an infant church functions within the most critical stage. Sheaves for Christ offers special care by offering property funds to these churches in their critical stage of existence.

The United Pentecostal Church International Ladies Ministries through Mothers Memorial funds provides Family Emergency assistance to home missionaries. Funds are available through the Home Missions Division to those who qualify according to the policy created by the combined work of Ladies Ministries and Home Missions.

Of special significance is the literature fund provided by Ladies Ministries. First-year missionaries receive a complete set of More to Life Bible studies and as many tracts as they need for outreach. By providing tracts and Bible study materials needed for evangelism, tools are made available to home mission churches for greater missionary activity.

Home Missions Statistics

While 10 percent of the churches exist in home missions status, and growth has consistently been realized, the statistical need for evangelism in North America remains staggering. Of the United States and Canadian population, only one person out of every 100,000 has been effectively evangelized with the gospel message; this means that of every 100,000 people, 99,999 are yet to be reached. Many communities still have no church proclaiming the complete gospel message. Millions still wait for the United Pentecostal Church International to bring a church to their community.

The United Pentecostal Church International is committed to respond to this staggering responsibility; working together with each other and with God, we believe the goal of reaching every person with the gospel is possible.

Summary

The Home Missions Division of the United Pentecostal Church International is observing tremendous results in the endeavor to evangelize all peoples in North America. The specialized endeavors of Home Missions are blossoming under God's hand of blessing.

The primary focus of Home Missions, the starting of churches, has enhanced the growth of new churches in many communities of North America, and these churches not only add to our outreach on this continent but also strengthen our ability to send missionaries to nations around the world. Missions is the work of the total church, and it begins at home.

Test Your Knowledge

1. What is the primary thrust of the United Pentecostal Church International Home Missions Division, and what are the positive implications when home missions is successful?

2. List the special ministries of the Home Missions Division.

3. List reasons why Home Missions is experiencing its greatest day of opportunity.

4. Offer at least three ways God displays His special pleasure on the planting of churches.

5. What are the means by which Home Missions efforts are funded?

6. What other divisions contribute to the work of the Home Missions Division?

Apply Your Knowledge

1. To determine the present ratio of churches to population in your community, obtain a list of churches from your Chamber of Commerce, multiply the number of churches by seventy-five (or a number that represents the average church-seating capacity), and compare the figure with the total population in the community. The difference will indicate an average number of people who do not attend a church of any denomination.

2. To determine the percentage of Oneness Pentecostals in the community, take the total attendance number, the total number of members
   from all the Oneness Pentecostal churches, and
   then divide the number by the total population
   in the community. You may be surprised at the
   answer.

3. How does giving to Sheaves for Christ and
   Mothers Memorial help start new churches?

4. Name several programs directed by the Home
   Missions Division.

Expand Your Knowledge

To expand your knowledge and understanding
of the Home Missions Division of the United Pentecostal Church International, you may wish to read
the following material:

- *If I Can Do It Anybody Can!*
- *Advanced Church Planting*
- *Organizing for Growth*
- *Exploring God's Word* Teacher's Manual

You can obtain a complete listing of Home Missions materials by contacting the Home Missions
Division (*homemissionsdivision.com*).

Around the World 12

And he said unto them, Go ye into all the world, and preach the gospel to every creature.
Mark 16:15

Start with the Scriptures

Matthew 28:18-20
Mark 16:15-16
Luke 24:45-48

John 20:21
Acts 1:8; 13:2-4
Romans 10:13-15

The founders of the United Pentecostal Church established as its motto "The Whole Gospel to the Whole World." In so doing, they acknowledged a God-given obligation to propagate the preaching of the gospel to all men everywhere so that all would hear the gospel and have the opportunity to believe in Jesus Christ and receive salvation. (See Romans 10:13-15.)

One of the principal reasons for establishing a church organization is to form a structure for individual believers and local churches to proclaim the gospel beyond local communities, state, provincial boundaries, and even national borders to "the uttermost part of the earth" (Acts 1:8).

As a constant reminder of this biblical purpose, the logo of the UPCI was artfully inlaid in the highly polished terrazzo floor at the entrance to the World Evangelism Center. The very name of our beautiful headquarters also testifies to all that this church admits a responsibility to "the whole world."

What motivates such a gigantic goal? Why should we, collectively as a church and individually as believers, proclaim to the world that we accept a worldwide responsibility?

We are "moved with compassion" as we see the physical, moral, and spiritual conditions in our generation. We believe that the gospel effectively changes these conditions (Romans 1:16). We believe that we are commissioned by our Lord to minister the gospel to every person (Mark 16:15). We believe that those who accept the gospel message will be saved.

It was Christ's love that caused Him to see the people of His day as sheep without a shepherd and to be "moved with compassion" into action to meet their need. Should His people, indwelt by His Spirit, His representatives in the world today, be any less moved to action to meet these needs?

The Conditions of the World

Physically, much of the world's population lives in poverty. Adequate food and shelter are beyond the reach of a great percentage of the world's people. The media remind us constantly of famine, pestilence, disaster, disease, and death among sectors of humanity. We who live with more than enough material goods find it hard to relate to the physical sufferings of vast populations. But as children of God, we must not allow ourselves to become calloused, unrelated, or unconcerned about natural hardships that pertain to the natural man.

Moral depravity is evident in our generation. Moral delinquency plagues every level of human society. Romans 1:21-32 describes the sordid moral condition of lost humanity. The only effective antidote for sin-enslaved people is the gospel of Jesus Christ, for its regenerative work brings a change in the nature of people.

Although one may find and clothe the beggar and possibly refine his morality to the point that he becomes a contributing member of society, without the gospel he remains without God. He is without hope until he experiences a new birth that produces a new nature and that makes him a child of God.

In view of the physical, moral, and spiritual condition of our world as we see it through eyes anointed by the love of Christ, let us consider our responsibility as Christians.

The Commission of the Church

During the brief years of His earthly ministry, Jesus chose and trained twelve men. By doing this, He prepared for the fulfillment of His purpose for coming into the world—making an atonement for us by His death on the cross. As He died on the cross, Jesus said, "It is finished." That is, the atonement was finished, but the work of the church had only begun.

After His resurrection, Jesus appeared to His disciples to commission them to evangelize the world. He said, "Go ye into all the world, and preach the gospel to every creature" (Mark 16:15). He proclaimed to them that "repentance and remission of sins should be preached in his name among all nations" (Luke 24:47).

From the mount of ascension, He commissioned His followers to be "witnesses" of Him at home (Jerusalem), in the next province (Samaria), and even to "the uttermost part of the earth" (Acts 1:8). There was to be no limiting boundary on the preaching of the gospel. The commission is not given just to a few persons called missionaries but to the whole church, to every believer who is a part of the church.

If we are to call Him Lord, we must do what He has commanded. We must accept the commission as our responsibility. Necessity is laid upon us to proclaim the gospel to everyone.

Our Commitment to the Commission

Responsibility for world evangelization was accepted by our church founders. To this end, the Foreign Missions Division was one of the two original divisions of the new organization. Other divisions were added as the organization matured and grew, but foreign missions was viewed as one of the principal priorities of the organization, and it is imperative that this divine task be the responsibility of every person who is a part of the church.

The Message of Missions

The message to the world is the gospel of Jesus Christ. About four of every five people in the world live in non-Christian oriented societies. They follow religious teachings of Buddha, Confucius, Mohammed, beliefs in the unknown spirits of the nature world, and many others. Most other religions allow the creation of images to be worshiped. Even some of those who call themselves Christians have so corrupted biblical Christianity that they do not know who Jesus is, why He came into the world, and what He will do for them now. There is a famine of the real bread of life—the Word of God.

Both by precept and example, we must introduce Jesus to people who have not heard of Him. We must lead them to confess that He is not just *a* god but the *only* God. Only after they come to recognize that they are sinners and that only Jesus can save them from their sins, will repentance of sin and identity with Jesus in baptism become meaningful.

God is faithful to confirm His Word as He did in the early days of the church. The baptism with the Holy Spirit is evidenced by speaking in unknown tongues, and those who receive this work of regeneration are truly changed. They turn from darkness to light, and they seek to conduct themselves as true representatives of Jesus. Often their commitment to Christ comes at a great personal sacrifice, sometimes suffering from persecution.

The Method of Missions

"How shall they hear without a preacher? And how shall they preach, except they be sent?" (Romans 10:14-15).

The UPCI charged the Foreign Missions Division with the administration of the church's witness abroad. This embraces 94 percent of the world's more than six billion people. It is an awesome charge. To succeed in any measure requires the support of every believer and every local church. The Foreign Missions Division can progress toward its goal when people and finances are made available.

The Foreign Missions Division is led by the general director of Foreign Missions, who is elected by the general conference of the UPCI every two years. Three additional executives serve full time with the general director in overseeing the executive administration of the foreign outreach of the church: the secretary, the director of education and associates in missions, and director of promotion.

143

The Foreign Missions Board consists of the four administrative executives, the six regional directors, and eleven pastoral members appointed by the General Board and ratified by the general conference, plus two district Foreign Missions directors elected by the district Foreign Missions directors. These appointed board members are pastors who willingly meet in session about twenty-eight days annually to provide direction, oversight, and control of this major enterprise of the church.

A district Foreign Missions director is elected in each district in North America. This district director is charged with representing the foreign missions cause to the churches, pastors, and laymen in his district. He is also responsible for scheduling the travels of deputizing missionaries to churches in his district.

The world outside of North America is divided by the Foreign Missions Division into six geographical regions for administrative purposes. A regional director cares for the missionary work in his region, traveling within his respective region to give encouragement, instruction, and oversight.

As the church grows and matures in each mission field, it is organized with the goal that it will develop into a national United Pentecostal church with national ministers assuming national leadership roles.

More and more of the national United Pentecostal churches are assuming a missionary responsibility to send their own people as missionaries to unevangelized areas. This expanding network of missionary endeavor has rapidly spread to more than 170 nations, making the UPCI one of the fastest-growing Christian movements in the world.

The Men of Missions

The key to success or failure is the missionary. While every believer has a responsibility to the commission of Christ, there are a select few whom the Lord of harvest calls to minister to another nation. The Lord instructs the church to recognize and to send these missionaries. The apostolic precedent is found in Acts 13:1-4. God calls; the church sends. Then the missionary goes with the unction of the Holy Spirit.

Applicants with their families present themselves to the Foreign Missions Board before they are recommended for appointment. Those recommended by this board are referred to the General Board of the United Pentecostal Church International for appointment. After they are appointed, they are commissioned by the general superintendent at the annual School of Missions. As the church supports them with finances and prayer, they are sent to the nation of their call to proclaim the gospel of salvation to all.

There are four categories of missionary appointment—career missionary, intermediate missionary, vocational missionary, and associates in missions. These categories cover individuals with and without ministerial credentials, long-term and short-term commitments, and vocations in various secular fields.

The Ministry of Missions

The commission to preach and teach is the all prevailing work of missions. The gospel must be preached and believers must be taught (Matthew 28:19-20). In the broader scope, it includes everything that pertains to the evangelization of the nation, including establishing churches, Christian schools, and Bible colleges, organizing and supervising the national ministers and churches, and providing literature in the language of the people.

The missionary must evangelize. He is to present the gospel to the unsaved. However this can be done in a given cultural situation, it must be done. Without converts, the work cannot progress.

The missionary must teach. Newborn children of God need teaching. Foreign converts need training to be true examples of biblical Christians even in the midst of unchristian surroundings. They must be established in the faith so that they will stand alone if need be.

Missionaries must promote the planting of churches. In the early stages of a field, the missionary may have to start churches himself. Later, he will train national workers to share their faith with their countrymen, and these national ministers will open new churches among their own people.

Missionaries must train workers. The productive missionary multiplies his ministry by developing those who learn from him (II Timothy 2:2). To this end, the investment of time and money is made in foreign Bible schools where thousands of national students are trained yearly. Most of these trained students become ministers among their own people. This is one key to the rapid growth of the church abroad.

The missionary must establish the local churches. By precept and example he must lead the national pastors and their congregations toward becoming a mature church. Children need teaching. Ladies need to become a contributing part of the church. The young people need training to become Christian workers of the immediate future. The people must be grounded in the truth in order to assume responsible roles in the church. The missionary needs to establish the church in both organization and doctrine.

Because most missionary work is performed in non-English fields, the missionary must develop basic literature, both for the purpose of evangelizing the lost and for training. It is imperative that young Christians have sufficient literature in their language to propagate and defend their faith.

146

The missionary must be the sum total of everything it takes to make the mission succeed—organizer, leader, financial administrator, builder, and motivator. He must have his goals well defined. He must be willing and able to delegate responsibility to other capable individuals. He must be willing to decrease as those he works into position increase. If he is successful, in due time he will work himself out of a job as missionary to that nation.

The Means of Missions

This is where the "sending" ministry becomes part of the total work. Whereas the Lord calls a few out of the body to be missionaries, He instructs all the body to "send" them.

The UPCI makes the "sending" of God-called missionaries a matter of sincere commitment. Every believer is asked to give unselfishly, sacrificially, joyfully, and consistently in order that missionaries might have sufficient resources to carry on the task in their fields of ministry.

Partners In Missions (PIM). This plan links the going missionary with the sending church. As the local church collectively pledges to finance part of the missionary's budget, it identifies with the missionary as a partner. The supporting church also identifies with the work of the missionary and prays for his ministry. The church rejoices over the report of those saved and learns about the mission field and its progress.

For his part, the missionary receives the needed finances and prayerful support from the churches. He has the assurance that, though separated by thousands of miles, he is remembered in prayer, will be supplied with the monetary necessities, and is ministering for the total church body.

Faith Promise. The individual can identify with the foreign outreach of his local church through making a promise by faith to regularly contribute an amount to the foreign missions offering of the local church. From the monthly faith promise offering, the church supports its pledged Partners In Missions through the Foreign Missions Division.

The faith promise commitment is generally made in response to an annual local missionary emphasis. The faith promise is generally made for the next twelve months until the next annual emphasis.

Faith promises for foreign missions are to be given willingly and cheerfully and with a measure of reasonable sacrifice. God blesses this kind of stewardship with overflowing measure. (See II Corinthians 9:7; Luke 6:38.)

Missionary deputational ministry. The outgoing or furloughed veteran missionary spends a planned period of time traveling among churches at home as part of his foreign missions assignment. In the churches, he reports on the work on the mission field, ministers to the people, and solicits both prayer and financial support.

The coming of a missionary to a local church is a time of excitement, something special on the church calendar of events.

When the missionary has raised the financial support for his budget, he prepares to depart for his field of labor. He meets with the Foreign Missions Division for an updating of the work on the field and for any further assistance he may need.

Compassion Services International. This aspect of the Foreign Missions ministry serves the physical needs of people on foreign soil. It provides an avenue through which benevolent funds can be channeled to provide relief of human suffering in areas experiencing famine, disaster, and disease.

Often it enhances the spiritual ministry of the church by providing food, clothing, medical services, aid to orphans, and assistance with education, agrarian development, and sanitation according to James 2:15-16, I John 3:17-18, and Matthew 25:40-45. In ministering to the needs of natural man, our missionaries exemplify the true compassion of Christ.

An annual sacrifice offering for the work of Compassion Services International is received on the last Sunday of February. However, offerings for this ministry are not limited to this one day. Funds may be sent to the Foreign Missions Division throughout the year. These offerings are over and above the regular support for the missionary and his ministry. Compassion Services International funds are distributed through the missionaries and national church leaders in each area of need.

Conclusion

As we enter the twenty-first century, the world of this generation presents the greatest challenge the church has ever faced. Temporal, moral, and spiritual conditions call for the solution found only in the teachings and provisions of the gospel of Jesus Christ. To this end, Jesus Christ has equipped and commissioned His church to proclaim Him to all men everywhere.

The UPCI created a structure for cooperative effort to fulfill the great commission of reaching other nations with the gospel. The program of the Foreign Missions Division reaches every believer in the local churches, for missions belongs to us all.

Test Your Knowledge

1. What is the motto of the UPCI?
2. What are the five "M's" of missions?

3. What are the "ministries" of missions?

4. What are the various "means" of missions?

5. What plan of finance links the missionary with the churches?

Apply Your Knowledge

"For unto whomsoever much is given, of him shall be much required: and to whom men have committed much, of him they will ask the more" (Luke 12:48). This verse of Scripture challenges us to do more with what we possess—both of knowledge and of means. This chapter instructs us as to how we can be of genuine service to the work of God in foreign nations.

Expand Your Knowledge

To aid you in better understanding the foreign missions endeavor of the UPCI, you may wish to read the *Foreign Missions Insight*. It can be ordered from the Foreign Missions Division, United Pentecostal Church International, 8855 Dunn Road, Hazelwood, Missouri 63042-2299 USA. This book not only contains information concerning the organized missionary outreach but also gives information regarding each missionary family and their field of labor.

The Church in the Community 13

Let your light so shine before men, that they may see your good works, and glorify your Father which is in heaven.

Matthew 5:16

Start with the Scriptures

Genesis 18:20-33;
   19:12-29
Proverbs 14:34; 29:2

Matthew 5:13-16;
   22:37-39
II Corinthians 5:19-21

"There are no absolutes—neither black nor white, neither right or wrong, neither heaven nor hell." These words, often spoken in the classrooms of American colleges and universities, condition students to alter moral values in life's situations. This philosophy, known as "situation ethics," teaches that moral rules are not absolutely binding but may be modified to accommodate any specific situation.

The religious community, however, does not ascribe to this erroneous philosophy of no absolutes. Churches are comprised of believers who are devoted to the authority of Scripture, expressing faith by their lifestyle that the Word of God proclaims the unchanging principles of Christian responsibilities.

"Righteousness exalteth a nation: but sin is a reproach to any people" (Proverbs 14:34). In a day when many things are changing—from natural surroundings to lifestyles—it is encouraging to know that Christian believers continue to function as a bulwark against evil influences. (See Isaiah 59:19.)

The force of Christian principles and righteous living should never be underestimated. It is recorded that one Sunday afternoon in Chicago a group of ballplayers entered a saloon. When they emerged, they saw a group of people playing instruments, singing gospel hymns, and testifying of Christ's power to save from sin. Memories of a log cabin in Iowa, an old church, and a godly mother raced through the mind of one of the ballplayers. Tears came to his eyes. Presently he said, "Boys, I'm through; I'm going to turn to Jesus Christ. We've come to the parting of the ways."

Some of his companions mocked him, but others were silent. Only one encouraged him as he turned from the group and entered the Pacific Garden Mission. Later the ballplayer told what occurred. "I called upon God's mercy. I staggered out of my sins into the outstretched arms of the Savior. I became instantly a new creature in Him!" And it is said of Billy Sunday that his conversion and preaching was the cause of numerous saloons closing their doors for lack of business. The power of God is lifechanging.

Why the Church Exists

What is the ultimate purpose of the church? Why does it exist? Why did God design and leave the church in the world? These questions deserve to be answered, and they are best answered by taking a close look at the people who make up the body of Christ on the earth. The church really exists to carry out two basic purposes—evangelism (to make disciples) and edification (to teach them). These two functions answer two questions:

- Why does the church exist in the world?
- Why does the church exist as a gathered community?

The church exists to act as an avenue through which God can deal with an unbelieving world. Jesus told His disciples, "Ye shall receive power, after that the Holy Ghost is come upon you: and ye shall be witnesses unto me both in Jerusalem, and in all Judaea, and in Samaria, and unto the uttermost part of the earth" (Acts 1:8). Evangelism is a primary reason for the existence of the church in the world.

The church exists as a local gathered community to serve as an avenue through which God can teach and edify His followers. (See Ephesians 4:11-16.)

The church is international in scope and mission, but it is also localized in congregations and ministers who delight in serving the needs of individual people. The United Pentecostal church in a community is therefore part of the worldwide endeavor to proclaim the gospel of Jesus Christ. The church's mission encompasses the whole world, but it is the local congregation that stands as a "flagship" to give direction and lend support to those who need and desire its services.

The church reaches. The impact of the church is often underestimated. Many people rely on the church only when they are in need of special services such as weddings and funerals. Yet the church makes the community as a whole a better place to live because of the godly influence that is projected through the church body. "When the righteous are in authority, the people rejoice: but when the wicked beareth rule, the people mourn" (Proverbs 29:2).

The Scriptures, speaking of the believers, state, "Ye are the salt of the earth. . . . Ye are the light of the world. A city that is set on an hill cannot be hid. . . . Let your light so shine before men, that they may see your good works, and glorify your Father which is in heaven" (Matthew 5:13-16).

The United Pentecostal church in a city may be named "First Apostolic Church," "Calvary Tabernacle" or another suitable title. Nevertheless, no matter the name, the United Pentecostal church is an asset to its community. Its members are law abiding citizens. They are good neighbors; and their desire is to be friends with all and to see others blessed with health, happiness, and success.

Abraham is a vivid example of what can happen when a person responds to the call of God and reaches out both to God and to his fellowman. When Lot and his family were defiled by the sin and iniquity of Sodom and Gomorrah, Abraham reached toward God and interceded in Lot's behalf, praying for him and his family to be delivered before destruction came to the inhabitants of the cities. Had it not been for the prayers of this godly man who knew how to trust God for victory, Lot and his children would have perished in Sodom.

Reaching toward friends. The pastor of the local United Pentecostal church congregation is a vital part in the endeavor to proclaim the saving gospel of Jesus Christ. He ministers to and guides the congregation in exciting areas of Christian service. But he is more than a "preacher"; he is also a friend in time of need. In fact, the Scriptures aptly describe the role of the pastor and church members as ambassadors. (See II Corinthians 5:19-21.)

Certainly the pastor is to be an ambassador or emissary for Christ. But the exciting news is that every Christian is also a representative of Christ and desires to fellowship with other people who love truth. To live in a community day after day and week after week necessitates the maintaining of human relationships. Many of the New Testament converts came from a society that involved a lifestyle unbecoming to a Christian. With their unsaved friends in view, Paul admonished Christians to "give none offence, neither to the Jews nor to the Gentiles" in their social life. "Whether therefore, ye eat, or drink, or whatsoever ye do, do all to the glory of God" in order, Paul stated, "that they may be saved" (I Corinthians 10:31-33).

Often "missionaries" are thought to be those people who dedicate their lives to proclaiming the gospel to people of other nations. However, every member of the United Pentecostal Church is a missionary on a mission to reach friends with whom he can share the beauty of salvation's plan.

When a parent reaches for a child, the communication is enhanced when the child responds by reaching back. In fact, children sometimes say, "I want to hold you," when in reality they want to be held by their parents or grandparents. A sincere hunger to be close to God and receive the blessings the church affords encourages the relationship of friendship and heightens the excitement of belonging to something worthwhile. The United Pentecostal Church International is reaching for people, and its members are thrilled when someone reaches back in response.

The Church Teaches Right Living

Clean lifestyles are practiced by the people who make up the United Pentecostal Church. Accepting and believing the life-changing experience of salvation,

Christians desire to live in a manner that is pleasing both to God and to their associates.

Family togetherness is advocated, and the church provides numerous activities that assist in promoting harmony in the home. The United Pentecostal church in a community offers a selection of wholesome services and activities in which family members participate together. It also provides activities for various age levels of family members. Sunday school classes for every age from nursery through adult levels are staffed with teachers and assistants who really care. Many of the churches sponsor Boy Scout groups, junior and youth Bible quizzing, children's programs, youth and adult outings of different kinds, adult fellowship groups, choirs, and other activities. In addition, the church usually offers a vibrant youth service in which the youth not only participate but also are in charge of the service.

The church teaches that people should be honest, pay their debts, be faithful to their jobs and loyal to their employers, be hospitable and courteous to others, obey the law, respect persons in positions of authority, and support worthy community projects. The church also teaches that members should dress modestly and decently, abstain from the use of tobacco, alcoholic beverages, and illegal drugs, and refrain from overeating to the detriment of one's health.

Christians are not to participate in immoral activities. They are not to be thieves, liars, or people of violence. Neither are they to commit sexual sins of any nature. God saves us from sin, not to continue living in sin. The Christian is to pursue that which is wholesome both morally and spiritually. Sin brings only distress and trouble in this life and after this life eternal destruction. Righteousness bears the fruit of peace and joy now and eternal life beyond the grave.

The Church Serves Others

The United Pentecostal church serves its community by providing activities for people. Youth programs often include wholesome recreation and entertainment such as scouting for those in the community.

Some congregations offer the services of a day-care center staffed with qualified Christians. Other congregations provide Christian schools for kindergarten through grade twelve. These schools usually follow guidelines to promote quality education under dedicated and qualified instructors, all in a Christian atmosphere.

Some church members teach home Bible studies or participate in home fellowship circles. Nursing homes are often included in the outreach ministry and services are conducted on a regular basis. Prison ministries provide opportunities for some church members to give their time and Christian witness to inmates.

Many times an entire family needs the services of a local congregation. Events such as weddings, funerals, and hospital confinements are prime examples when families appreciate the ministries and facilities of a local congregation.

The Church Teaches Neighborliness

The United Pentecostal Church believes and practices the "royal law": "Thou shalt love the Lord thy God with all thy heart, and with all thy soul, and with all thy mind. . . . Thou shalt love thy neighbour as thyself" (Matthew 22:37, 39). A person who enjoys the benefits of friendship must first show himself friendly.

The "golden rule" has often been set aside by people who were more interested in selfish pursuits.

But members of the local United Pentecostal congregation are taught to believe and practice, "Do unto others as you would have them do unto you."

The pastor sets the example of "neighborliness," leading the way for others to follow. As ambassadors of Jesus Christ on the earth, the believers—pastor, church leaders, and all others—are energetically interested in the well-being of each person. Every church member is considered a personal missionary to share the "good news" of the gospel and to encourage all to be a part of the fellowship in the church.

One man in the Bible responded to Jesus by asking, "And who is my neighbor?" Jesus answered with the story of the good Samaritan, indicating that a person's neighbor is anyone who is in need of assistance even if that person is unknown. (See Luke 10:25-37.)

The Church Teaches Citizenship

What is the civic responsibility of Christians? How can the church influence the political decisions that affect moral principles? The apostle Paul admonished the Thessalonians (and us) to conduct their business affairs in a proper manner. Some of them may have been using the teaching about the return of Christ as an excuse for being lazy. "Do your own business, and work with your own hands," Paul admonished, and then he gave the reason why: so "that ye may walk honestly toward them that are without, and that ye may have lack of nothing." (See I Thessalonians 4:12.)

Christians should live responsible lives in the community, and their responsibility extends to making the community a better place in which to live. More and more the people who comprise the congregations of the UPCI are becoming interested and involved in community affairs. Some serve on city councils, public school boards, special committees, state agency appointments, and even in federal governmental positions. In a democracy, it is needful for Christians to be informed about the affairs of government and to participate by voting in elections and corresponding with elected and appointed governmental leaders. The extent of their involvement, however, must be carefully limited to Christian activities and Christian principles.

The members of the UPCI are encouraged to fulfill all the obligations of loyal citizens. The following quote from the Articles of Faith emphasizes this desire: "The Word of God commands us that first of all we are to pray for rulers of our country. We, therefore, exhort our members to freely and willingly respond to the call of our government except in the matter of bearing arms. When we say service, we mean service—no matter how hard or dangerous. The true church has no more place for cowards than has the nation. First of all, however, let us earnestly pray that we will with honor be kept out of war."

Respect for authority and those who serve in leadership positions, both secular and spiritual, is a characteristic of a true follower of Jesus Christ. Even Jesus admonished, "Render unto Caesar . . . " the things that are due. United Pentecostals respect the authority of those who enforce the laws of the land and those who serve in the courts of the nation. Godly principles dictate that every individual do his best to live in a manner that is pleasing both to God and mankind.

Test Your Knowledge

1. Why does the church exist in the world?
2. Why does the church exist as a "gathered community?"

3. How can the church be both local and international in scope?

4. What kind of influence does the church have in a community?

5. How can a local church reach out to new people who need Christ?

6. How can the church serve both its members and other people?

7. Is the church influential in the affairs of governments?

8. Are Christians ever exempt from obeying the laws of the land?

Apply Your Knowledge

It is desirable for Christians to become more aware and involved in their community. Make a list (indicate priorities) of the functions in which you can or would like to participate.

Think of ways you can also win or make new friends.

List ways to enhance your Christian witness.

Expand Your Knowledge

Consider reading magazines or books that relate to the role of the church in our world. The *Pentecostal Herald* is an excellent source of current and inspiring information. Become more aware of community functions that you could either participate in or attend. Be informed! Speak out! Be a part of God's greatest gift to the community—the church.